Briar
COTTAGE

MY SUMMERS IN A TOWN CALLED GIMLI

JOE MACKINTOSH

 FriesenPress

One Printers Way
Altona, MB R0G 0B0
Canada

www.friesenpress.com

ISBN
978-1-03-912604-6 (Hardcover)
978-1-03-912603-9 (Paperback)
978-1-03-912605-3 (eBook)

1. BIOGRAPHY & AUTOBIOGRAPHY, PERSONAL MEMOIRS

Distributed to the trade by The Ingram Book Company

For Karen, Heather, and John

1950s Map of Gimli

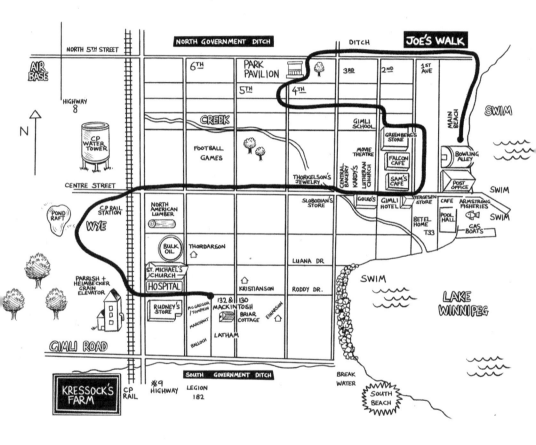

Reliving Adventures

Gimli is situated on the west side of the south basin of Lake Winnipeg, some 100 kilometres north of the City of Winnipeg. The community of Gimli has always been a magical place for me, and with good reason. The two separate lots at 130 and 132 Fifth Avenue, two houses now, was one big property in my family's era of cottaging, from 1934 to 1958. The little wooden bridge over the ditch at 130 Fifth Avenue is long gone. I can picture Dad putting it together: sketching a plan (he never started any projects without the drawing, knowing that he couldn't build it if he couldn't draw it); scouring the property and the surroundings for boards; visiting the shed; searching the containers for screws, or better still, bolts (a machinist to the core); fetching the hammer, hand saw, tommy bar, axe, spade and any other tool that might come in handy; and then building.

I found an old photo, probably from the summer of 1936. There's curly-haired Duncan, just turned four, with a hammer in his hand, and Mom, spunky as ever, putting the final touches to the bridge. Maybe it's set up. They showed up at the last minute for the photo, pretending they did the job, and Dad took that picture and then the next one. Mom is ferrying Duncan back to the cottage in the wheelbarrow. The bridge leads directly to the front door of the cottage in the middle of the lot at 130 Fifth.

My mother holding Spotty the fox terrier and my brother, Duncan.
Photo from the Mackintosh family collection

I'm here in the yard after all these years. This was the site of our family's Briar Cottage, named in honour of the wild rose bushes growing in the yard. I came every summer from 1942 to 1958. Much like the overflowing Gimli creek from the high-water springs of the 1940s, imagining the past has invoked a stream of memories. The property appeared to be much bigger in those days, but isn't that true of so many things long past? From a recent school reunion, I know for sure that my former junior high school—a building constructed in 1905—had bigger classrooms, hallways, and stairwells when I attended.

Spotty is buried over there in a shaded spot. Here's where the original cottage stood, and beside it, the bunker-like cement cooler where my brother, Ord, and I hand-mixed cement during construction. The outhouse and shed were back on the lane next to those blackberry bushes. They're still flourishing after all these years. The raspberry patch is gone. The berries were enormous and delicious, staked in three rows, reaching to the sky. It was like walking through a giant tunnel of berries. I can picture my summer pal, Glenn Rudney, strolling through, sampling the fruit on his way to our back door. And now, there's Leslie Einarson, another summer pal and member of our gang of swimmers, riding past on his bike.

Our lot next door at 132 Fifth had fewer trees, so it was used for tossing footballs, kicking soccer balls, batting baseballs, and chipping golf balls. I dug in a Campbell's soup can so Glenn and I could have a chip and putt game without the putter. My sister Marie was unintentionally batted in one of our baseball games. That caused a furor of excitement, a call to Dr. Johnson, and a trip to the Johnson Memorial Hospital for X rays.

The bonfires were lit just outside of our property, learning to ride a bike happened by pushing off the trees, and over here is where I tested my wrestling skills with Jeannie.

Only the scream of the T33s is missing. I'd look up, following the sound above, searching the sky, and then, well beyond the thunder, there was the plane already over the lake. It might have been Sigfred Hernes, one of many North Atlantic Treaty Organization (NATO) recruits. Sigfred was a young and single Norwegian pilot posted to learn the art and science of flying at the Gimli Air Base, preparing to defend his country from the threats of the Cold War. Fortunately, it wasn't all hard work and no play. Sigfred found a camper for a life-long partner.

The cottage, nestled in the trees of the inside lot, was a spartan paradise. There were few amenities. The building was a simple, uninsulated, wood-framed structure, there was an outhouse, and we used a cement bunker-like cooler adjacent to the cottage for milk and butter. Mom did all the cooking on a monster wood-burning stove acting also to heat the cottage in the cooler days. When Dad bought the property, the cottage was just a hut: a kitchen, wood stove, and bedroom. He tripled the space by constructing a living-dining area and two more bedrooms.

We fetched pails of water from a public artesian well just outside the corner of the property. Dad suggested bottling this well-water and taking it back to the city. It just tasted so good. He reckoned that all drinking water would eventually become scarce for Canadians and bottling this Gimli water would be a good business. The family wasn't as sure, but Dad was some sixty-five years ahead of the curve on the production and sale of bottled water.

It was also common for people to collect rainwater. Dad erected two large barrels for water storage. Next to that, he built a small outdoor washstand with a mirror attached to the house. To give some feeling of comfort, he printed HOT on one of the barrels and COLD on the other. It was an illusion, but it worked. There were no complaints about the temperature of the washing water.

I recall the joy of waking to the sounds of birds, a crackling fire, the whistle of the kettle, wood smoke, and the wafting aroma of the boiling oats. When it rained, there was the added comfort of hearing the patter, the rhythm of raindrops on the roof.

The original hut-segment of the cottage had a large four-by-twelve-foot screened shutter in the kitchen. Mom was oblivious to the heat of soaring summer temperatures. Cooking her scones and oatcakes, chocolate cakes and cookies was a priority . . . thankfully. She would get the fire roaring in the kitchen stove even on the hottest days of summer. Dad would come to the rescue and open the shutters, saying, "Let's get some cool air." Later in the day, if Mom had a sore neck, she would blame it on the draft of the open shutters.

There was a coal-oil space heater in the living room to supplement the heat of the wood stove when temperatures of late summer nights dropped. That room also had a series of prints of First Nation chiefs. Each was unique from the paintbrush of Scottish artist Adam Sheriff Scott. He was commissioned by the Royal Bank of Canada to provide this art for their 1940 calendar. Dad saved the pages, laminated them, and then fixed them to the walls of the living room.

In earlier days, there was no hydroelectric power in our cottage, and even after its availability, only the kitchen was wired.

Making toast became much easier to do after we gained electricity in the kitchen! The old method of sticking a fork in the bread and holding it over the hot stove was scrapped for an electric toaster. It took some getting used to. I can still hear the warning, "The toast is burning." Someone forgot to open the sides of the toaster and turn the bread so both sides were browned.

When the sun set, Dad lit the coal-oil lamps in the living room. Some were fixed on the walls, and others sat on tables. The routine of filling the lamps with oil and the pungent smell of the coal-oil lingers still. The lamps produced their flickering flame and yellow-ish light as if by magic. It was a cozy setting, especially on rainy evenings. There was undoubtedly little heat, but the amber light provided an illusion of comfort.

The combination shed and backhouse was on the west side of the lot against the lane. I can still see Spotty, our sixteen-year-old fox terrier, lying in the shed on his last days. He had wandered away for two weeks—what a worry for my mother—ready to die on his own terms. All our neighbours and friends were on the lookout. Jeannie Kressock found him in the ditch by the highway, settled down in the reeds, preparing no doubt for the next stage, dreaming of his adventures past with the rats: capturing them next door in the tall grasses, throwing them in the air, breaking their necks and depositing them on our cottage doorstep as a gift for his family.

After finding our dog, Jeannie picked up Spotty and took him back to the cottage. He had difficulty standing. Dad put him in a cardboard box lined with blankets. He slept in the shed, waiting for the end. I was around six years of age, awakened to a lone rifle shot that morning. The Mountie had been called. Maybe old Spotty had the right idea; find a soft spot in the reeds and dream of past exploits with the huskies, tied by Armstrong Fisheries plant waiting for their sleigh-pulling duties of winter. On several occasions, while walking with my dad, Spotty darted into the middle of the pack. There was a major ruckus. Moments later he would be out of the melee and the danger of the larger dogs, walking with his master—calm again—while the growling and scrapping of the husky pack continued.

The rain and Mom's tears came down in torrents. She'd already had her share of sadness. Good friends, Ethel and Jack, were down for the weekend so Ethel provided solace and her share of tears. Jack worked at the railway with my dad. Ethel and Mom were soul mates, usually the last ones partnered on the dance floor stepping lightly to Five Foot Two, Eyes of Blue. Not this weekend.

Mom would, from time to time, read the tea leaves in Ethel's cup. Friends and relatives who visited often requested a reading of the leaves—another reason for having a pot of tea at the ready. I never thought of it at the time. It was just something my mother did. Tell fortunes from tea leaves. People took it seriously. She was good at it.

Raised in the Highlands of Scotland, Mom, Madeline by birth but Maud to her friends, was undoubtedly subject to all the superstitions and folklore of her upbringing.

"If a black cat crosses in front of you, stop immediately and spit. Spit to defuse the pending bad luck of this beastie. 'No crossing under ladders' is a given. Don't even think of it. If you're checking out a full moon, make sure you have a few coins in your pocket. And don't be doing this moon gazing inside the house. Looking at a full moon through a glass window could give you no end of bad luck. And new shoes—don't come in the house and put them on a table. That's a complete no-no. On New Year's Eve, known as Hogmanay by the Scots, the first-footer, the first person to enter the home, should be tall and dark and carrying a lump of coal. If no one was tall, go for the darker guy. No coal, well grab a bag of something—anything—just don't walk in empty-handed. Otherwise, you're taking a chance on a year of bad luck."

Teacup reading seemed to come naturally to my mother. It was a divination much in demand.

She would make a pot of tea using only black tea leaves. I can't remember any other colour of tea in those days. There would be a scone or an oatcake or a biscuit to go with it. The teatime and resulting conversation seemed to take forever. Maud would take the cup, dispose of any liquid, and turn it over, letting the leaves settle and no doubt thinking of the conversation that just transpired. Then she would ponder the configuration of leaves, slowly and deliberately looking at the slanted bone china cup, puzzling on the orientation. All was quiet.

"Ah, yes, there's something there."

There were certain shapes that had meaning—a tree or a person or a winding road—all signs of both good news and bad. There was usually some good news—perhaps an unexpected visit from someone making contact with a lost friend or relation. There was a prevalence of tall and dark guys. Often there would be money—a welcome addition to the prognosis. But sometimes, I could tell that there wasn't much there—or worse, there was bad news—pending illness, perhaps. Here she became introspect and in her wonderful Scottish brogue would intone,

"Let's pour another cup and let it sit a bit longer."

There were tears of both joy and sadness. Sometimes the prognosis was happy, occasions where people enjoyed travel or unexpectedly received money, but there were also times when the black clouds of tea leaves predicted darker times—undefined misfortunes. Tea reading was more than entertainment. It was an opportunity to have a serious conversation with a close friend. Both Ethel and Maud had been through the highs and lows of life. Perhaps my mother was trying to soften the blow of sad news; news that surely had caught her by surprise, changing the course of her life. My mother had a mantra over the years that undoubtedly had helped her cope.

"You take the bitter with the better in this world, and over a lifetime, everyone seems to get their fair share."

"I remember playing in your yard on Fifth Avenue. Your Dad had left these spindly poplars but cut the grass between the trees. It was just so park-like. The little cottage was on the second lot, 130 Fifth, some- what offset in the trees. There was so much space and so many sparrows. All you could hear was the din of the singing birds. When I recall the sound of the birds, my mind returns to the fond memories of the yard." (Beverley Einarson, Gimli resident)

We entered the property off the lane on the north side of the black-berry bushes. The entry was framed by two towering poplars, goal posts for many of the games on that lot, the least treed of the two. When my brother Ord purchased his first car, a 1942 Dodge, Mom decided that she would like to drive. It was sometime in the early fifties, so she was in her forties. This car was a monster, built like a tank. It had fluid drive. You could shift directly from first gear to third—the precursor of the automatic. It was her first time out, and she was doing well, getting to know the routine of the clutch and gear shift. She also made the turn nicely into the yard but was somehow spooked by the poplars. She overreacted in steer-ing, turned sharply, and crashed into a tree. Perhaps she should have waited for power steering. The old poplar got the worst of the collision, but there wasn't a scrape on the Dodge. Mom got out of the car and said, "That's it for me." The experience was the end of her driving aspirations.

The poplars also bring back memories of looking after my sister, Marie. She's some six years younger than me.

My sister, Marie, sitting in the yard at the cottage, probably
just turned four years old that summer.
Photo from the Mackintosh family collection

It must have been the summer of 1953 when she and her summer pals, Larry Latham, the next-door camper, and Terry Anderson, the Gimli kid, liked to act out the Peter Pan saga.

She always took the lead role of Peter, a portent of things to come—jumping on a picnic table, challenging Captain Hook, brandishing her sparkling sword (a poplar-stick facsimile), leaping off the bow of the ship, and tumbling through the grass. Fortunately, this game took hours, since one of the things I had to do for my mother was looking out for my sister, making sure she hadn't wandered out of our yard. It was easy when the Peter Pan play was happening, but that didn't last forever.

Sometimes she would disappear unexpectedly, although it wouldn't have been unexpected if I had been watching.

I would get the call from the house. "Joe, is Marie with you?"

"Of course, she's right here."

She was here minutes ago but now had disappeared. Fortunately, I remembered her hiding spots. In her mind, she was often still in the Peter Pan game, and Peter was climbing high to look out for ships. I would check the broad-branched poplar tree and there she was, sitting high on a crook of branches looking towards the lake for Captain Hook. I would warn her that she was too high and tell her to come down. She would warn me of the crocodile hanging around the base of the tree and claim that she couldn't come down.

"I only know how to climb up."

She was lying, but her grammar and vocabulary were superb for a five-year-old. I would climb to where she sat and remind her to take her time coming down. Once she turned around, I would ensure that her foot was secure on the first branch. Then she would dodge past me like a flying squirrel, leap off the bottom branch of the tree, and scamper back to the house. I don't think the squirrel could have done it faster. Finally, I, too, would be back on the ground. Then, there was a call from my mother.

"Quit teasing your sister!"

Maybe I shouldn't have told her that she had to stay in the tree forever or remind her that there really was a crocodile lurking in the raspberry patch.

The poplars are also a reminder of my dad's tree removal projects. Removing dead trees or trees that looked like they were dying was one of the heavier chores. Even bigger, healthier trees that had the potential of falling on the cottage, outhouse, or shed were also under scrutiny. It was time to get out the rope, the axe, spade, and hand saws. "Hard work never killed anyone," he'd say. I never doubted the truth of this adage from my dad, but my unspoken opinion was, "Do we have to keep proving it?"

It's 1955. I'm thirteen years of age, in the backyard of the cottage,
axe in hand, ready for the next project.
Photo from the Mackintosh family collection

Trees were never cut by leaving a portion of the trunk with the roots still in the ground. The entire tree was removed. First, the roots were exposed by digging out the sod and soil. Once the roots were chopped through, the tree could be felled by pulling on the end of a rope, but first, the rope had to be secured to the tree. Yes, that was one of my jobs. I got to climb as high as I could safely climb to tie on the rope. It was a job I loved.

My mother wasn't always as happy. She would be watching our progress or lack of and just might appear to stop the fun.

"That's too high. He's going to fall."

All I heard from my dad was, "A little higher would be perfect."

Jeannie lived on a farm on Gimli Road. It was where I first learned that you could drink the milk directly from the cow. Her mother was milking a cow and she asked me if I wanted a drink. Yes, please. She squeezed some into a cup and handed it to me. What a shock, it was warm—a revelation for me.

On another day, my brother, Ord, and Jeannie's brother, Johnny, decided to ride the pigs. Jeannie and I were spectators. Ord was sitting on the fence, and Johnny, still dressed in his "going to church" clothes, was in the pen, intent on riding. He grabbed one of the animals around the neck and leaped on. The pig was bucking and squealing, trying to shake him off. Johnny kept his grip until the pig stopped suddenly and Johnny slipped off into the mud. The sty wasn't the cleanest of rodeo sites. Johnny was now chasing the other pig when his father shouted from the door of the house, "Johnny, get out of there."

There was one summer when I was keen to test my strength. It was 1952, the summer after I'd completed the fifth grade. I'd grown in height now almost as tall as my friend Jeannie. I played sports and figured I was ready to take on the world.

She and I had raced, biked, swam, and played Red Light Green Light, Mother May I, and Knock Off Ginger. I wondered if she wanted to try wrestling.

I'm sure she was confused. She lived on a farm, hoisting pails of milk and bales of hay and probably knew down deep that this would be a short match.

I knew that girls didn't wrestle—at least they didn't back in the fifties. I hadn't seen any on CBC's Saturday Night Wrestling. I figured it would be an opportunity to try out a little trick I had learned.

During school recess, my friend Gavin and I would fight for fun—boxing and wrestling. It was a typical boys' contest. Even though the sparring was play, there was a deeper motive. In the pecking order of guys, our school chums, we were trying to figure out who was tougher—Gavin or me? Here was an opportunity for me to try out a few of my fighting moves. To be fair to myself, I described the manoeuvre to Jeannie in advance.

"If you are lying on your back and your opponent is sitting on your stomach, pinning your hands behind your head, I know how to get free."

She said, "You do? How does that work?"

I said, "Easy. Just tighten your stomach muscles and then flip up your body. Surprise is the key."

Jeannie took off her jacket and said, "Let's try it. Get on your back."

"Not so fast, Jeannie. First you have to get me on my back. Then you have to hold me down. That's the hard part. I'm not going to just let you get me down."

Jeannie was taller than me, but I figured because she was a girl, I would automatically have an advantage over her. That's probably why I challenged her with such confidence. Anyway, I had spent a winter sparring with Gavin.

"Sounds good," says Jeannie. "Let's go."

Instantly, she had her right arm around my back and her right leg across my legs. Then she torqued me, and I was off my feet and immediately on my back on the ground. It happened so suddenly that I didn't have time to react. It took just seconds. She must have been wrestling the pigs on the farm. Now she was sitting on my stomach and had my hands pinned behind my head. I was hoping my mom or dad or my sister hadn't seen this happen. It was embarrassing. Boys are supposed to be stronger. Jeannie was tough.

"So, now try your move. Show me how it works," said Jeannie, leaning in close and whispering.

I had already tried it and I couldn't budge her—absolutely no movement. I shouldn't have tipped her off about the move. I tried it again. Nothing.

"Joe, why don't you try the move that your friend showed you?"

What could I say? I had already tried it, and nothing happened. There was so little reaction that Jeannie didn't even know I had tried it.

I waited and gave a mighty heft of my bum. Again, nothing. I couldn't budge Jeannie.

"Okay, let's get up," I said.

"No way," said Jeannie. She was having too much fun. No wonder she liked wrestling. She was good at it. "You gonna say 'uncle,' or you gonna try that half-assed move again?"

I sure as hell was going to say "uncle"—eventually—but lying here wasn't such a bad option. And anyways, she was in control. I would get up when she let me up. Perhaps Jeannie's hormones were firing. Mine weren't, not yet. Give me time and a little more testosterone in the veins. My body was just beginning to enjoy the soft and cuddly comfort of the opposite sex, but my mind was still focused on getting on with all the cool things that could be happening—throwing a ball, kicking a ball, catching a ball, hitting a ball, dribbling a ball—did summers ever get any better? And then, to the rescue, my pal Jack from across the lane was beside us.

Jeannie got off me, slowly, hopped on her bike and rode away grinningly, savouring her victory.

"You okay, Joe?" said Jack. Jack Tompkin was my neighbour, fellow camper, and long-time friend. He stayed at his Grampa McGregor's cottage across the lane on the corner of Sixth Avenue

Silence. I was feeling lousy from my wrestling defeat, but I sure as hell wasn't telling him.

"What kinda game you guys playin'?" said Jack.

"I was showing Jeannie some defensive moves, like how to get out of a wrestling hold when someone's pinning you."

Silence.

"I think she just put you in a piss," said Jack.

"You feel like tossing the football?" I replied.

The campfire site was on the boulevard, just north of the entrance. My sister, Marie, was around seven years old when she took charge of inviting neighbours to a Saturday night bonfire. Our parents didn't have any idea that they were hosting a party. Marie would

be playing with her friend Donna, Jack's sister. She would take the opportunity to invite Donna's parents and her grandparents, Neil and Sarah McGregor, and anyone else that might be there at the time.

"We're having a ceilidh and a bonfire tonight, and you are all invited." Of course, it was a surprise to our mother. Then she would move next door on Sixth and give the same message to Joe and Jean Marchant and their daughter, Audrey, if she were down. Joe was a long-time pal of my dad, referred to as "old Joe" to distinguish from me, young Joe. He and Dad emigrated from Scotland together. I'm sure that Joe would have winked at Marie and asked if her mother knew of this party scheme.

"Of course, she told me to invite you." Then one more call on Sixth Avenue, to Charlie and Amy Balloch. Like Neil McGregor, Charlie, too, worked for the railway at Weston Shops. They began their life in Gimli as campers, but once Charlie retired, that's where they made their home.

The party was on. Donna's mother, Ioline, would consult with my mother. There was undoubtedly a trip to either Rudney's Store or Tip Top Meats for wieners and buns and a stop at the Central Bakery for jam busters and icing cookies. Ord and I would dust off our accordions, Donna would take out her dancing shoes, and Donna's dad and brother Jack would tune up their fiddles.

We would begin with a few Scottish tunes: *I Belong to Glasgow, Muckin o Geordie's Byre, A Hundred Pipers*, and one of my mother's favourites, *The Northern Lights of Old Aberdeen*. Jack and I would play a kolomyjka, a staple tune at local Ukrainian weddings. Then the chorus was ready to belt out the campfire standards, like *Home on the Range*. Donna would dance the Sailor's Hornpipe. Once the fire was on, Charlie would wrap potatoes in foil and stuff them at the bottom of the fire. He would also take charge of preparing the hot dogs. For me, Charlie set the standard. I'm sure he was just adding mustard to the buns, but the taste was spectacular.

There's something about certain foods that trigger memories. On one occasion, my mother baked a chocolate cake. She iced it, and I ate at least half and paid for the overindulgence. I was sick to my stomach for the next twenty-four hours. Perhaps it had nothing to do with the cake. Maybe I'd experienced stomach flu or excessive amounts of sun, but it took years to clear that memory. When I have chocolate cake today, I'm back in the cottage on Fifth Avenue, reminding myself not to overeat chocolate cake.

As fall approached, we would seek out the bulrushes. They grew profusely in the ditch by the Parrish and Heimbecker grain elevator on Highway 9. After a day of drying, the ends were dipped in coal oil. The lit end was a perfect torch for the campfire. The local Mountie would slide by in his cruiser to say hello and remind us to put the fire out and to consider our sleeping neighbours. We assured him there were no worries on that front. All were here.

"I don't think they're going to make it tonight."

> (Madeline Mackintosh, sitting on the 5:20 train prior to departure from Winnipeg, waiting for her husband Mack and his work mates from CPR Weston Shops.)

Rail was the way many cottagers got from Winnipeg to Gimli and back, at least until 1957. There was a magical quality to that experience. The coal-fired engine sat like a nervous racehorse frothing steam, eager to get going. The locomotive provided its own mechanical mystique—the sight of the wisps of smoke, the smell of the burning coal, the sound of the haunting horn, people milling about the station. Many were Canadian Pacific Railway workers with passes. They were fair-weather migrants from the big city, eager to soak up the light and heat of summer along the beaches of Lake Winnipeg.

I can't say my mother shared such awe. She and Marie and I would be sitting aboard the 5:20 train in the Winnipeg CPR Station on a Friday afternoon waiting for my dad and his mates to get on board. They got off work at five o'clock at Weston Shops and had twenty minutes to catch the train. It was downright nerve-racking for my mother. She was always sure they were going to be left behind.

Mom, Marie, and I would take a leisurely ride down on a Logan Avenue bus, but the men would be on a more frantic ride. Three or four of the camper-guys would share a taxi to the station. The skilled driver would wind his way eastward between the tracks and Logan Avenue to Higgins and Main Street. Sometimes the train would be pulling out of the station, and they still hadn't appeared. Perhaps Mom was right. This time, they were too late. But inevitably, minutes later, there they were, surprise, surprise—laughing at the worried looks on their families' faces.

"You didn't think we'd miss it, did you?"

They had hopped on the last car and walked through the coaches. My mother let out a sigh of relief.

There was much anticipation during the winter and early spring months for our return to the lake. We never waited for July and August and the assurance of sunny weather, mosquitoes, and fish flies. Everyone was always keen to get down as early as possible to get started on the new season. The May long weekend was the date that campers opened up the cottage, cleaned out the cobwebs, took off the shutters, aired things out, flipped the mattresses, and for me, reconnected with my summer friends. Sometimes the ice would be off the lake—not completely gone but at least out a bit from the shore—and then the cry, "Can we go swimming?" would rise, with the standard parental reply, "Don't be crazy; the ice is still out in the bay. You'll get the chill of your life."

There were a number of trains between Winnipeg and Gimli in the late 1940s and early fifties, perhaps as many as four per day on the weekends. For excursions to the cottage in spring or fall prior to my two-month summer stay, we would catch the 5:20

Friday train and return on the seven o'clock evening train on the Sunday night.

The steam engine was slow to get up to speed. There was both an engineer and a fireman in the cab of the locomotive. The fireman's primary job was to feed the fire with coal.

Unlike the steady acceleration of a diesel engine, the steam engine would lurch for the first few yards, jolting unevenly until the flow of steam steadied. But as the locomotive got up to speed as the fireman shoveled more coal, there was the gentle rocking of the cars, the steady beat of the engine and the clacking of the rails. The hydro poles sped by. The window was open, and there was that great smell of coal burning as the steamy-smoke floated by. It was always fun to have your head out, but that was short-lived as Dad reminded us of the danger of getting a cinder in the eye.

"Tickets, please."

The train conductor, the man with the golden stripe on his cap as opposed to the white stripe of the train-man, arrived to punch a hole in our passes and place a little tag on the window blind. Dad always carried his pass in his wallet, which covered both him and my mother. It was a permanent long service document. The kids were issued passes for individual trips.

Next was the Newsy with his standard call. "Cigarettes, cigars and chocolate bars—cracker jack, chewing gum and candy."

He also sold newspapers and sandwiches which we never bought. We had my mother's baked goodies for a journey that took a little more than two hours. The conductor would call out the stops prior to the station: Matlock and Whytewold, with the long wooden piers extending into the water; Ponemah; then Winnipeg Beach with its endless boardwalk, rides, games, and the wooden-structured roller coaster; Boundary Park, home of the historic border of New Iceland and Manitoba; Beachside; then Sandy Hook, home of Moe Doyle and the Sandy Hook Golf Course; Husavik; and finally, Gimli. The 5:20 ended its journey at Riverton.

The rail station was just north of the highway at Centre Street.
The water tower is seen north of the station. A windmill located
at the harbour was employed to get water to the tower.
Photo courtesy of Dilla Narfason

Gimli passengers got off. Mail bags, passenger bags, boxes, and pets were unloaded from the baggage car. If this was only a weekend sojourn, we had nothing to collect from the baggage car. All our possessions were stored in the overhead rack. If instead, we were here for the two-month summer stay, Spotty, our fox terrier, was with us. He had to be caged in the baggage car, an affront that was appeased with a rare meal of baby-beef liver.

We walked back to the cottage, hauling our bags. First, we went south down the cinder trail adjacent to the track, then east on Luana Drive past Bailey's Esso bulk oil station on the north and St. Michael's Church on the south, then a right turn and south on Sixth Avenue, past the back side of the Johnson Memorial Hospital, and finally, the short walk east on Roddy Drive to the back lane, the entrance to our summer home.

If my parents were still around today, they would be confused with the street names, a relatively new innovation for the town. If visitors were coming down by train, we would meet them at the station. People coming for the first time by automobile needed directions, something like, "When you see the Parrish and Heimbecker grain elevator, you're almost there. Get ready to make a right turn at the grocery store and then turn in at the lane between Fifth and Sixth Avenue."

It never took long to get back into the rhythm of summer once I reconnected with some of the local kids, permanent residents of Gimli, the enthusiastic actors of adventure. Retrieving my bicycle from the shed was high on my list of priorities. It was a typical clunky-looking cottage bike with a wire carrier, a necessity for grocery runs. It was designed for an adult, a relic of the past, heavy: made of iron and built to last.

Leslie Einarson and his family lived on the corner of Fourth Avenue and Roddy Drive, just a block east of our cottage. His dad, like his Icelandic ancestors, was a commercial fisherman. He fished year-round, using a gas boat in summer and an ice fishing camp in winter. A horse and sled would pull out the camp: a big kitchen, beds, bunks, and couches. Leslie's dad and uncles would stay out on the ice for three or four days, pack the frozen fish, and then harness the huskies to haul the boxes over the ice to Armstrong Gimli Fisheries.

Leslie would be riding his bicycle past our place—probably on his way to Rudney's Store—the same friendly guy then as he is now. "You're back!" That broke the ice for another year. We would be seeing more of each other swimming at the docks. His accident never slowed him down.

Then Glen Rudney would ride over. His parents ran the store on the highway just minutes from our cottage. As the summer progressed, he and I would bike everywhere, ride the raft on the pond near the train station, swim at the docks, play every sport imaginable, and see ninety percent of the movies at the Gimli Theatre. We were also ardent pinball players.

After our water escapades at the harbour, some of the swimming gang would make their way to Sam Toy's Gimli Café on First Avenue. That visit usually happened in the morning. It was never too early for a few fries and maybe a Coke. Sometimes Sam was still outside, sweeping the sidewalk. He always appeared happy to see us, even though we weren't big spenders.

"You guys staying out of trouble? You want some chips? Be careful on the floor. I just sprinkled it with the green stuff."

We would head directly to the pinball machine, put our nickel in and get playing. Intent to guide the ball in the right direction, we began to move the table. Suddenly, Sam was on us.

"Don't rock the pinball. If you do, I'll kick you out."

Bob Thordarson lived a few blocks down the street on Sixth Avenue, the current site of the Gimli Car Wash. I would meet up with him at the dock on our swimming adventures, but it didn't take many years before Bob was distracted with a better alternative. He met Carol.

Ed Suchy, another permanent resident of Gimli, lived farther north on Third Avenue, just over the ditch and into Loni Beach. His home was close to the Gimli Park and Pavilion, and that's where we would see each other. He and his brothers, Tony and Dave, were busy making a dollar delivering papers and cutting grass. They were a hard-working crew but also appreciated the lighter side of life.

There was one day when Ed figured that grass cutting was the perfect way to meet girls. He was cutting a lawn with a motorized gasoline mower in Loni Beach. It was a hot day, and Ed was observing several girls just coming out of the water. At first, they didn't appear to notice the grass cutter. It didn't matter. Ed was already pondering a walk to the beach afterwards to say hello.

Then, to his delight, the next time he turned to mow back in the direction of the water, the girls were waving. Yes, he would be heading down to the shore after this job for sure. He kept watching them, and they kept waving. Ed turned to cut in the opposite direction and at last looked down at his mower. There was another reason for the waves: the girls were trying to get his attention. The engine was on fire.

Looking back, my most remarkable memory is how time stretched across an infinite summer. September and the beginning of a school year was too far away to imagine. There were endless things to do even if the same things were repeated every day in a timeless playlist of activities. Swimming at the dock, many times a day, was at the top of that list.

> *"I sure remember the fun we had in the water—playing tag on the fishing boats and diving off the wheelhouse of the tall boats like the Goldfield. You wonder how someone didn't break bones running on the slippery decks or scampering up the sides of the gas boats?"* (Leslie Einarson)

Our favourite location was the harbour between the large pier and the smaller dock. Today's pier is just a longer version of the one from the 1950s. The dock is still there too; the fishers' boats are still tied in tandem during the off-season.

*The Gimli harbour taken from the little dock looking north
west towards Armstrong Fisheries and the main pier.
Photo courtesy of Dilla Narfason*

The large pier hooked over towards the dock with an opening of some 100 metres. It was big enough to accommodate the large fish-haulers, such as the Goldfield and Barney Thomas and the SS Keenora, a dual-use cargo and passenger ship. Gimli Armstrong Fisheries was located at the harbour adjacent to a red shed nearer the water. It undoubtedly had a purpose other than a launching platform for the swimming gang—divers and belly floppers.

The local gang of swimmers, sometimes two and often over twelve, would gather on the dock. Bikes rested on the south wall. In July, the large fishing boats, known as gas boats, parked three abreast along that dock.

Our first priority was to jump or dive into the water. The harbour was dredged periodically to accommodate the larger boats. I'm not sure of the depth, but it was well over our heads. Then we would swim the 100-metre channel to the pier and climb the

Joe Mackintosh

ladder. Often, we would head diagonally across the harbour and end up at one of the chutes of the pier. The chutes were inclined planes built into the pier to assist in unloading boxes of fish. On sunny days a swimmer or two—often girls—would be tanning on the chutes. This was an opportunity to shake some water on them; it was a time to discover that the girls had a different sense of humour than the guys.

Sometimes, if a larger fishing vessel was docked, we would climb on board and make our way to the upper deck. You had to be ready to jump or dive back in the water. Deck hands were on your trail.

"Didn't you see the *No Trespassing* sign?"

"No."

Splash!

In my early swimming days, there was always a warning from my mother to keep safe, especially when I was off to the dock. Our fifth-grade school class took swimming lessons at the YMHA in Winnipeg. I passed all of the requirements and received a piece of paper to prove it. I made sure I took the paper with me to Gimli just in case I needed to verify my capabilities to my mother. One of the requirements was to be able to tread water for ten minutes, a key pre-requisite for entering the waters of the harbour. Not everyone that swam at the dock had taken lessons or even, for that matter, could swim.

I remember a young guy, probably only seven years of age, showing up. He went to the edge of the dock and jumped in. As he struggled to stay afloat, it became clear that he wasn't a swimmer. In a matter of seconds, he had sunk twice under water. When he surfaced, I hauled him back to the dock. He took a short breather and jumped back in. This time he was calmer, moving his hands and leaning back to tread water. It wasn't perfect, but he was staying afloat. He had learned how to survive in the water by trial and error. He stayed calm. Sink or swim; it was a metaphor for life's challenges to come. I expected to see him back, but it was a one-day

24

occurrence. He probably figured, "Hey, I know how to swim. Time for a new challenge."

There was another incident, a prank, really, all in good fun except for Mike Michaluk. Mike, who lived on a farm on the outskirts of Gimli, was taking a walk on the pier. He hadn't planned on going in the water. He wasn't wearing a swimsuit. There was a local gang of swimmers—tanned and fit—treading water and diving under like dolphins. Mike made his way to the side of the pier, curious to see who was in the water. That's when someone came up behind Mike and pushed him in. Perhaps the pusher assumed that Mike could swim. He couldn't. He was fully clothed—shoes and all.

Leslie Einarson was watching this drama unfold. Fortunately, Mike didn't panic and turned on his back. He was floating successfully but appeared to be moving out to the middle of the harbour. Les jumped in, swam to Mike, grabbed him by his jacket, and towed him to the safety of a ladder.

Usually in the mid-afternoon, our family—most often my sister and brother and I—would head east from our cottage to the lake, a short five-minute walk. Sometimes my dad would put on his suit. It was an opportunity for him to demonstrate the Inverness crawl. This was an efficient side stroke that he and old Joe perfected as youths in the Moray Firth of Scotland. My mother would make an appearance in her bright yellow suit once per year. It had to be an extra hot day. As a non-swimmer, she would splash about near the shore.

1953 on the breakwater at the bottom of the road. From the left: Jack Tompkin;
Joe; my sister, Marie; and Donna Tompkin Goodman
Photo from the Mackintosh family collection

The town built a breakwater known to our family as "the dike" along that stretch. We would climb over the wall to a small parcel of sand to access the water. There were better beaches. Both South Beach and the main Gimli beach were wider and deeper in sand, but this spot, referred to as the "bottom of the road," was the fastest route to the water from our cottage.

A view of construction of the breakwater on the south side of the harbour. The building is the Betel Home. After swimming at the dock, we would bike the trail past the Betel verandah. Some of the residents, happy for the company, would reach out to touch us on our way by.
Photo courtesy of Dilla Narfason

Gimli always had a huge expanse of beach on the north side of the harbour, a beach that is still popular today. My gang of swimmers were seldom there. Instead, on high-wave stormy days, we sometimes swam on the north side of the pier. In retrospect, it was a dangerous place to be, especially when the north wind roiled the water and high waves slashed the sides of the pier. The fun was in surviving the onslaught, staying far enough out from the jetty, preventing your body from meeting the concrete, surviving the storm . . . as foolish and dangerous as that sounds. I never told my mother about those days.

Pounding waves on the north side of the Gimli pier in August of 1951.
Archives of Manitoba, George Harris fonds, 1979-141, Album 20 page 13.
"Gimli Harbour", August 1951, P7453

Of all the places in Gimli, the main beach appeared to be the safest place to swim. The depth of the water increased gradually; there was a sandy bottom and there were no currents to pull you out, at least on the calm days. Despite such safe conditions, there were still dangers. People have drowned in all depths of water, as Jack Tompkin and I can attest. He and I and his Uncle Marty were there one evening sitting on the beach enjoying the sunset and the cooling breeze from the water. Marty had just purchased a new 1956 Dodge with push-buttons for changing gears. He had taken us for a ride.

Suddenly there was a commotion. Someone on shore was calling for help. His friend had gone out—perhaps no more than 100 metres—and was on his way back to shore, but then disappeared. There were no beach lifeguards on duty at this time of day.

Uncle Marty, the Canadian Navy veteran of WWII, went into action. In minutes, he had his shoes off and his pants rolled up and was making his way to the water. It took some time to figure where the swimmer went down but once the approximate location was established, Marty advised the other five rescuers to hold hands and form a circle. The hope was that someone would step on the body and eventually—after minutes that passed like hours—someone did. They pulled him to the surface of the water. His face was a bluish colour, his body limp. The volunteers held him upside down to drain the water. The police arrived on the scene. They began giving him artificial respiration. The ambulance arrived. Medics stepped in and continued their life saving procedures, but after close to two hours of trying, the unknown swimmer couldn't be revived. He was covered with a blanket. There was no rush now. The rescue team rested. They had done their best to save him.

It wasn't the first drowning in Lake Winnipeg at Gimli, but it was the first time that Jack and I had witnessed one. It had happened so quickly. It took only seconds. The water wasn't even that deep. When the crisis ended, there was a long lag before people stood to leave. There wasn't any sense of voyeurism. It was more a vigil where the spectators were still locked in hope—some in prayer—that this drama would end well. Now everyone was trying to cope with the reality of what happened.

There were happier occasions. Thanks to Harry Kressock, Jeannie's dad, one of the joys of summer was our annual trip to Winnipeg Beach. We would gather at the farm, and Harry would load us in the back of his one-ton truck. There were bales of hay, something to lean on and perhaps cling to since the deck was slippery and the back of the truck was open. I can't remember anyone riding with Harry in the cab, so there would be six of us in the back. Roads were more gravel than tar and Harry drove cautiously, probably doing some fifty kilometres per hour. It seemed to take forever to cover the sixteen kilometres, adding a further sense of anticipation and excitement. There was lots of chatter about getting there:

which rides would we go on first, who doesn't like cotton candy, how can we get a prize from the ball throwing, how many times will we be able to ride the rollercoaster?

There were always crowds of people walking the boardwalk, especially on a Saturday. A noon-hour passenger train with its engine idling would be sitting at the station.

I would get a dollar or two from my parents to spend on the rides, but Harry was always checking to see if we had enough money to keep the fun going. The dodgem cars were a huge hit. We would always repeat that ride. Then we would lose some money on the machines, especially the one with the crane that was intended to pick up plushy bears and metal trinkets. "Did you see that? I was so close." There was some scoffing at the merry-go-round. As the years evolved, it appeared too tame, especially with the presence of dads or moms riding and clutching their toddlers. In the end, we, too, jumped on the wooden horses and held tight to the reins; a ride was a ride.

The major event was a ride on the roller coaster, a big rambling wooden structure built in 1919 and modified in 1924. The old cars would slowly rattle their way to the top, almost twenty-five metres. It seemed to take forever. Everyone was quiet. My mind was lulled into the false assumption that "this isn't so bad," but that feeling changed during the pause at the top—the calm before the storm as the cars were readied to make the descent to the bottom. There were shouts and screams. Arms were raised as the cars picked up speed. There was a sense of fear combined with ecstasy as we approached the turns. I could feel the dips in the ride and the fear that the old structure was giving way. One of these times, this car wasn't going to make the turn, but fortunately, it always did, and at the end of the ride there was always a cry of "Let's go again." And that's what we did.

Then Harry would drive us back to Gimli. It was a quieter ride basking in the fun we'd had. There was a touch of sadness knowing that it would be another year before we again made the trek by truck.

I was fortunate that my dad worked for the CPR. He and I would be catching the train some Saturday morning from Gimli to Winnipeg Beach for the annual company picnic. The crowd of railway families and their kids would gather in the open field across from the station. I would run in the races. Charlie Balloch was always in charge of the ice cream booth. At the end of the day, he would pack up the few leftover revels, popsicles, and dixie cups, store them in his dry ice cooler, and haul them back by train to Gimli. Most of the stock ended up with our family. Our underground cooler wasn't cold enough to keep them frozen, so lots of iced goodies were consumed that day.

Charlie was quite the force in our summer community.

Charlie Balloch was a proud four-foot eight-inch Scot, born and raised in Peterhead in Aberdeenshire, Scotland. He wore a cap—not quite a tam but close to it—much like a Brit might wear in his open MG roadster. The cap was always perched or cocked at just the right angle. He wore his trousers high over his waist, greatly reducing the distance between his waist and neck. Braces were standard fare. He never drove a vehicle. When he walked to the shops in the centre of town, Charlie put on a white shirt. He lived south of us, just down the lane on Sixth Avenue.

Charlie was a blacksmith at CPR Weston Shops in Winnipeg and surely looked the part. He retired in the early fifties and became a permanent resident of Gimli. Now he could spend all his time growing flowers, an activity that was formerly only a hobby.

He loved working the soil and was famous locally for his garden full of dahlias. When his rainwater ran out, Charlie and his wife Amy—a skinnier version of Charlie—would truck carts full of water from the corner well. He had such a beautiful and prolific garden that he began to sell flowers out of his greenhouse. Local residents and campers flocked to his home.

Charlie was also generous with his time and talents. In 1956, Branch 82, the Gimli Royal Canadian Legion started construction on a building to house the club. It was and still is located just south of Charlie's former home on Sixth Avenue. Charlie Balloch was a major contributor in the construction of the building. I can still see him on the roof doing some of the sheeting. Construction was completed in 1957 when my brother and I helped Charlie and others carry in the billiard table for the downstairs clubroom. On Saturday nights in the summer, my mother and friends often attended bingo in the upstairs hall where one of the Beauchemin brothers, Lionel or Mickey, would be calling out the numbers.

Charlie was also known as a guy who would pitch in to help when friends and neighbours had a project going.

In the late forties, Neil McGregor, who owned the corner lot on Sixth Avenue, decided to build a cottage. My dad drew up the rough plans. Neil set a weekend date to begin construction, and word of the project went out to the neighbours and Neil's sons. On the weekend of construction, Dad and the rest of the neighbours showed up at the site with their hammers, saws and ladders ready to build.

I was only some six years of age and not wearing a hard hat as I walked through the construction site. Someone above called for a hammer. Ord picked one from the toolbox and tossed it up. The recipient missed the catch. The hammer came down and hit me on the head. Blood trickled down my face. Everyone rushed to my side, so I cried a little to make the most of the attention. My mother suggested a trip to the hospital but my dad—given his role as a first-aid attendant at Weston Shops—figured I received just a glancing blow.

Around noon hour on the second day of the project, the McGregor boys arrived. Surprised, they said, "You started without us." They lauded the progress and then headed off to the beach. Their priorities were beach and girls first, helping Dad second. They were soon back, much to the surprise of the volunteer builders, wondering how they could help. Their Dad jumped on the opportunity.

"The hole has to be dug for the outhouse," said Neil.

An outhouse or backhouse was the only option for sewage disposal in those early days at Gimli. In polite company, the structure was known as a privy: a small building having a bench with holes through which the user may defecate or urinate. Everyone dug a seven-foot hole and built a little house over it. Some people built two-holers, just in case company were down and there was a run on the facilities or in case two female friends wanted to make it a social occasion—time to go but also a time to chat.

There was a more practical reason for two-holers. In theory, it would take twice as long to fill the holes compared to the standard one-holer. The exercise of re-digging the hole would be postponed.

We had a two-holer at our cottage and there was only one occasion that I remember when there was simultaneous occupation.

Sisters Anne and Helen and their husbands were at our cottage for the weekend. They decided to go together one night in part because it was dark and felt they needed the company—safety in numbers—and in part to catch up on family gossip.

For some reason, Anne was fiddling with her newly acquired diamond ring, pulling it off and on. Perhaps it was a nervous habit or maybe the ring was too tight on her finger. Sister Helen decided to give her some advice.

"Don't be fussing Anne, especially in here. You don't want to drop it."

Such is the power of suggestion. Anne fumbles the ring and drops it. Yes, she drops it into the nasty abyss below.

They went back into the cottage and told their story.

"You dropped it where?"

After much fossicking in the dark, flashlights and long sticks and metal strainers were assembled, and the ring was retrieved.

Neil decided on the one-holer. The boys got on to the digging job and after two hours, the hole was taking shape—three feet square and one foot deep—only six more feet to go. It was a hot day, and this was a tiring job. It was an auspicious start, but it was time for a drink break and maybe a swim. Time to head off to the pub for a tumbler or two of cold beer and then down to the main beach for a dip.

"We'll be right back."

There was another of life's unfulfilled promises. As the day went on, the unfinished biffy hole sat in the sun and the tools of the trade—the axe for tree roots and spade and shovel—were idle. Undoubtedly, the boys were having too much fun. It was a hot day; they had day jobs to earn money for their university education and this was a short weekend opportunity to relax a little. Both of them had served overseas—one in the army and the other in the navy—so they were cool about how they should allocate their time. They had probably met women on the beach and were lining up their evening entertainment.

Charlie was unsympathetic. He had been walking back and forth along the lane checking the digging progress, and so far, there wasn't any. On his last tour of the site, he couldn't hold back any longer. He leaped into the hole, picked up the spade and started digging, furiously. He kept digging for the next two hours until you could only see the top of his cap bobbing up and down. Finally, my dad convinced him to take a break.

Dad fetched a folded step ladder and set it up on the side of the hole. Clearly fatigued, Charlie climbed out and headed home. Dad jumped in and took over where Charlie left off. He was finished the job in some twenty minutes and ready to put down the shovel when the boys arrived back from town.

"Wow, Mack, you've been working!"

Charlie took a special interest in my wellbeing—sometimes with excessive exuberance.

After a swim at the dock, the swimming-gang would sometimes visit the pool hall. We were too young to play at that time but still enjoyed watching the better players. There would be the standard games of pool or billiards and games of pea pool and poker pool happening. It was harmless entertainment; at least, that's what we figured. But not Charlie. He must have been standing by HP Tergesen & Sons across the street, because one day he saw me leaving through the front door of the pool hall to First Avenue. He told my dad this wasn't a place for young lads like me. We didn't need the bad influences of billiard players. My dad took a different approach. It's one that I've come to fully appreciate.

"You can always walk away from trouble."

He trusted my judgement. Pool was a good game. From then on, I entered and exited from the back door.

There was another occasion when my pals and I gathered on a rainy day to play bingo in our cottage. Mom and my sister had returned to the city to assist my dad—do some laundry, scrape the kitchen plates, cook some meals, vacuum, and generally return the city home to respectability.

To make the bingo game more exciting, we would each place a penny in the middle—if we had any—so the winner would receive a five-cent pot. We were having a good game until Charlie showed up. He knew I was alone, and he was checking on my status. I knew I was busted when Charlie sidled up to the dining room table and saw the pennies.

"Okay, boys, put away the coins. Gambling is illegal. You could get into a lot of trouble with the Mounties."

I know what all of us were thinking.

Hey Charlie, don't have a conniption. We're playing for pennies. There's only twenty cents among the four of us.

We kept quiet. Charlie was the unofficial warden, keeper of the principles of morality and self-appointed referee to keep me on that Presbyterian path.

It kept raining that day—the day of the infamous game of bingo—and the back lane behind our cottage was becoming boggy and rutted, treacherous for vehicle traffic. I was having my supper when I heard some commotion out back. A car was stuck in the mud, and it was disappearing further into the swamp as the motor continued to rev. I recognized the driver. It was The Airman, Charlie's neighbour. Charlie didn't like the guy, so he never referred to him by his name. Perhaps there were a few late-night parties, incidents where Charlie passed judgement on his lifestyle. The Airman saw me standing in the yard and shouted over.

"Hey Joey, would you mind if I used a few of your logs to put under the back tires? I'm digging myself into quite a hole here."

I wasn't sure how he knew my name. Perhaps there were sympathetic vibrations between us since we were both under Charlie's watch.

I knew that Charlie didn't get along with the Airman and I was hoping that the stuck car would be gone before Charlie realized what was happening. I knew what Charlie would be thinking.

These partying animals deserve their fate. Play with the devil, and eventually you get to join him. It serves you right. Your car is stuck in a bog.

We hauled several logs from our wood pile to the back of his car. He positioned them in the mud in front of the back tires and got back in the car, and after a bit of jigging and jogging he was able to move it forward out of the bog. The Airman got back out, thanked me and we began to remove the logs from the lane and pile them back in our yard. That's when Charlie came storming out.

"Joe, don't give that bugger anything."

The Airman ignored Charlie. He just kept working on the logs, hauling them back into the yard. He looked like he, too, had been lying in the lane, covered in mud from head to toe. Charlie was still fuming.

"Look at the mess you've made. Why the hell are you coming down here in weather like this?"

The Airman came over to where Charlie was standing and said that he hadn't meant to make such a mess but was in the middle of the lane before he realized how difficult it was to get through. If he'd known how bad it was, he wouldn't have attempted this route.

Charlie was red in the face and clearly irate. He moved closer to the Airman—a guy that was over six feet tall, in good shape physically and probably forty years younger than Charlie. Charlie made a giant leap in the air, swinging at the Airman's chin. Not that I laughed, but there was a lot of humour in the incident. There's under-five-foot Charlie trying to punch this tall guy, and he almost hits him. Fortunately, the Airman's reflexes were good, and he moved his head back to avoid the punch. He put his hands out and backed away, saying, "C'mon, Scotty, take it easy. Calm down. I'm only trying to get home."

Charlie ranted about the noise and the fact that the Airman's gate was broken, and he hadn't fixed it. The Airman apologized for any past bad behaviour that had riled Charlie. Charlie turned and went home. The dude winked at me and hopped in the car.

It must have been difficult living as a neighbour to Charlie. His lawn was immaculate. The flower beds were full of dahlias. He had an industrial-type gas mower, one of the first to have forward and reverse gears, and loved to cut grass. Charlie not only managed the grass cutting on the boulevard in front of his home but also those properties running north for the next three lots.

He also took on some local jobs of tree cutting and gardening. There was some money involved, but Charlie just liked to help people, so the money was secondary. There was one job that was a little too much for one person—even for Charlie—so he asked if I would help.

The job was at Whippoorwill Cottage, Thirty-four South Colonization Road in South Beach, the home and property of Miss Florence Harris. Her father, Percy, had built the cottage, and being a high school English teacher, she spent her entire summers in Gimli.

Florence bought her flowers from Charlie and often hired him to do yard work. On this occasion, she had hired Charlie to remove a large old oak tree from her property—roots included. Off we went one early summer morning to do the work. The tree was enormous. It took us a week to do all the cutting, raking, and hauling of wood. Again, this was an era before chainsaws, so the two-man pull saw, axes, and a small Swedish saw were the tools at hand. Charlie, over sixty years of age at this point, was in great physical condition. I was fourteen years of age that summer and there was no way I could keep up with him. The week was one of the hottest, so we were thankful for the fresh cookies, lemonade, and Wynola Cola drinks.

This was also the summer when a good friend of my parents arrived from Outlook, Saskatchewan. Her name was Jo McKay. Her husband had a leather goods business in Outlook. After he died, my parents always referred to Mrs. McKay as Jo from Outlook. That's the only name I ever knew.

She fit into our routine quickly. The only unusual thing for us was that she liked to wash up in the morning, topless, at the outside basin. One morning, my mother observed Charlie behind his fence in his backyard, peering down the lane. Mom told Jo about Charlie the early riser and suggested that perhaps she should be a little more discreet.

"Why? What's the big deal? The cat can look at the Queen."

She was right, and no one argued. Jo continued her topless ablutions. After a two-week stay, Jo returned to Outlook. We held a little party for her on the last day of her stay. Charlie was there and told Jo how much she would be missed. Charlie, honest to the core.

On Saturday nights, Charlie would invite the neighbours over to watch television. Being a full-time resident, he had a television, a luxury that the cottagers didn't have. It wasn't a matter of just watching television. Here was an invitation to watch Saturday Night Wrestling. It was the highlight of Charlie's week. Amy would put out the buttered scones, and Charlie would uncork the Ballantyne's whiskey.

Charlie was a huge fan of Saturday night wrestling. The matches were staged for entertainment as the first priority and wrestling the last—even though there was no doubt as to the skills of the wrestlers. Most people accepted the staging. Charlie was an exception.

He was glued to the television but often leapt out of his chair to admonish either the mean wrestler or the referee. One of the bad guys—perhaps Mad Dog Vachon—was doing his dirty tricks routine, grabbing the hair of his opponent Whipper Billy Watson or doing something equally unfair behind the referee's back.

"He'll get his comeuppance; his goose will be cooked," said Charlie.

It was more fun watching Charlie than the wrestling spectacle.

Television reception in the early days was poor. There was often a foggy-snowy screen, and storm clouds were sure to take out the reception. Charlie figured that a new and bigger aerial would do the trick. It was the only option.

My dad, Joe Marchant, my brother, and I arrived to provide some assistance. Charlie was already on his roof, scampering from corner to corner to tie down the support wires. There was fear from his helpers that in his haste, Charlie would forget that he was four metres above ground and at some point, fly off the roof. Ord and I were told to hold the main mast until all other wires were in place. My dad and old Joe were on the other corners. Charlie was in charge and almost racing from corner to corner around the roof.

The job did get more difficult when, without warning, a storm materialized. The wind speed increased, and we were all hanging on to our positions with some difficulty. After a few minutes, the storm calmed, and Charlie was re-revved and clearly anxious to get this job finished. Then Amy called up from below.

"Charlie, Miss Harris is here to pick up her plants."

This is Miss Harris of the yard of giant oaks. Given my angle on the roof, I couldn't see her, but I could imagine her standing below dressed for the occasion in a flowing and pleated skirt, earrings, and a silver necklace. There wouldn't be a hair out of place—the very definition of kempt. She had a tinge of Victorian propriety, always addressing Charlie and Amy as Mr. and Mrs. Balloch. I'm sure there would be no rude behaviour in her classes. She was likely to be a tyrant for punctuality and decorum. We held our breath and waited for Charlie's response. He didn't lose a beat. This was not the time or place for matters of the garden.

"Tell her to bugger off and come back when we're finished this bloody job."

Perhaps in the heat of getting this aerial in place, Charlie hadn't realized that Miss Harris was standing next to Amy. If Amy was able to hear Charlie's instructions, so was Miss Harris. But I suppose Charlie didn't care. He was busy, and why would she come along now and demand flowers? Cracky! Didn't she know he was putting up a new aerial? Didn't she know that Little Beaver and his compatriots were on the wrestling bill tonight? Apparently not. Florence Harris was shocked.

"My Lord, what language, Mr. Balloch!"

In 1959, we visited the Ballochs at their new home in Kelowna,
British Columbia.
From the left: Joe; my mother, Madeline Mackintosh; my sister,
Marie Mackintosh; Charlie; and Amy Balloch
Photo from the Mackintosh family collection

Retracking History

My mother, Madeline, and her boys, Ord on the tricycle,
Duncan holding the wagon, and Spotty the dog in front of the
cottage at 130 Fifth in the summer of 1936.
Photo from the Mackintosh family collection

My dad, John Mackintosh, with Duncan on the fence.
The view is looking north on Fifth Avenue towards the centre of town.
Photo from the Mackintosh family collection

Dad had bought the properties 130 and 132 Fifth Avenue for $100 in 1934. He first visited the town in the early thirties and stayed in a cabin at the Tourist Camp—a wooded area with bunk-lined cottages and tents located between Fifth and Sixth across from our properties. Dad was known as a camper.

Today, seasonal inhabitants of Gimli—cottagers, in their lingo—are still referred to as campers by long-term residents of Gimli: people who rent accommodation, people who own simple cottages, people who have built year-round homes, used seasonally, like the snowbirds of Pelican Beach. My wife Carole and I have lived permanently in Gimli for almost twenty years, and I still think of myself as a camper.

When the campers leave at the end of the summer season, Gimli returns to normal. The town is quieter. There is less traffic on the streets. It's easier to park in front of the Post Office. The beach has solitary walkers, there are no line-ups at the food stores, the weekend partying subsides, parade floats are back in storage; and there are fewer cars on the roads.

My earliest memories of being in Gimli arise from being there with my grandfather, John Macdonald.

My Grampa Macdonald and myself in 1943 in the cottage yard. My dad had constructed outdoor furniture from poplar saplings. The bench is an example.

He came from Scotland in 1940, after my grandmother died, to live with us in our Winnipeg home. The sailing companies traversing the ocean couldn't give any guarantees that he'd make it across in the early days of WWII, with submarines lurking in the Atlantic shadows, ready to sink an enemy ship on command. No one was even sure when the ship was scheduled to arrive. Security measures were high. The family was continually checking arrivals at the eastern ports of Canada. My parents were unaware that he finally disembarked in Quebec City on July 31, 1940, but so relieved when he arrived by rail in Winnipeg.

Grandad had worked as a gamekeeper in Scotland so loved to get away from the life of the city to experience "roughing it" in Gimli.

I came to Gimli with my grandfather for a number of years in the mid-forties. We walked many miles together; or more correctly, he walked many miles while I was mostly pulled in the wagon, winding through the dirt roads of Gimli, listening but not understanding when he stopped in at the butcher shop across the road from Greenberg's General Store on First Avenue. There he spoke in Gaelic with one of the butchers, a Scot who was more than happy to pass the time with a fellow highlander and to converse in a Gaelic tongue foreign to the locals. Then we would pop into Greenberg's for a sample of candies, my Grampa's treat.

My mother, Madeline, hadn't seen her dad in ten years. Mom came to Winnipeg to marry my dad in 1930. She had a boyfriend in Scotland at the time. It was early in the relationship, but I'm sure Hamish had hopes that it would grow over time. Every Sunday they went walking in the town of Elgin. Mom was working in the Elgin Psychiatric Hospital as a student nurse. I can imagine the final goodbye.

"I won't be walking with you next Sunday."

"And where will you be then?"

"I'll be on my way to Canada. I'm getting married."

"My God. You're going where? You're getting married?"

Hamish was happy with Madeline's friendship and undoubtedly assumed that there was a future together for both of them. I suppose he also figured there was no rush—not a good assumption. He had no idea there was a Canadian suitor lurking abroad.

John Mackintosh, known as Mack, had emigrated to Canada in 1923. Serving in the Machine Gun Corp of WW1, he had returned to Scotland after the war to discover a dearth of jobs. Scotland was in a serious recession. Dad was a machinist, trained with the Highland Railway in Scotland. He heard of the opportunities for employment in Canada, boarded the SS Marburn in Glasgow, landed in St. John New Brunswick, took the train to Winnipeg, and began work with the CPR.

Dad and two of his WWI British Army buddies in 1917, prior to their service in Belgium. After the war, my dad John Mackintosh emigrated to Canada in 1923. Fellow soldier, Bill Wilson, pictured in the middle, chose instead to move to Cleveland in the United States. Addie Sutherland, on the left, returned to Inverness Scotland and spent the rest of his life there. Dad reunited with Bill Wilson when he and his wife travelled to Gimli in the summer of 1954.
He met with Addie in Scotland in 1965.
Photo from the Mackintosh family collection

The work of a machinist on steam engines was no different from his experiences in Scotland, but the Canadian weather—especially in winter—provided a different challenge. Mack was first assigned to work in the Round House in Ignace, Ontario, a major divisional point of the railway. The round building had rail entry and exit points around the circumference where the engines came in and out. The locomotive was parked over an opening—a pit—where inspection and maintenance work would be performed. In winter, when the engine came into the Round House, snow and ice was caked to the undercarriage. When there was time to allow the engine to sit, there was no problem, but more often a repair needed to be done in a hurry. In such times, the job of the machinist was doubly challenging. Mack recalled the challenges of focusing on the repair while shivering from the melt of ice and snow running down his neck and back.

On May twenty-fifth, 1928, Mack returned to visit his parents and his sister in Scotland. That's when he met Madeline at a café in Lossiemouth, a small town on the eastern coast of the North Sea close to Elgin. He took Madeline back to his childhood home in Inverness to meet his family.

Mack wanted Madeline to come back to Canada with him in 1928, but she needed time to think this through. Making a lifetime commitment to marriage and emigrating to Canada after a three-week courtship was not on. Mack returned alone to continue his work with the CPR in Winnipeg's Weston Shops but never gave up the correspondence, encouraging Madeline to join him in Canada. She finally agreed.

Coming to Canada to get married, Madeline Macdonald got across the Atlantic in steam ship Minnedosa, one of the smaller passenger ships in the fleet of Canadian Pacific in 1930.
Photo from the Mackintosh family collection

Madeline Macdonald sailed from Glasgow on the Minnedosa with eighty-seven passengers aboard. The ship docked in Quebec City, and once a Justice of the Peace and two witnesses were assembled, John and Madeline exchanged vows on June 15, 1930. After the service, they took a day trip to Montmorency Falls some twelve kilometres from Quebec City. Getting married prior to the trip back to Winnipeg was a sly and thrifty-Scottish trick. On return to Winnipeg, Madeline qualified for a rail-travel pass—free passage courtesy of the CPR.

My brother Duncan was born in 1932 and brother Ord in 1934. I came along in 1941 and my sister Marie in 1948.

Living through the 1930s wasn't easy. Work on the railroad for Mack was sporadic. The economy was in deep doldrums, and the

CPR was subject to those same ups and downs of the cycle. Dad was laid off work for a substantial period in late 1937, and the prospects of permanent employment as a machinist at Weston Shops were dim.

The family was living in a home in the west end of Winnipeg, making monthly payments to the owner—the plan being to eventually own the property —but the hours of work with the railway had been cut. Employees worked for ten days and then laid off for the next ten days. The lack of work and income meant that Mack couldn't meet the monthly financial obligation on the home. He felt that he needed to move the family to a rental property. It would mean walking away from a home where he had accumulated a respectable equity of ownership. The owner was empathetic and encouraged Mack to stay the course. The economic situation would eventually improve, but for dad, the burden of the debt and his inability to pay outweighed the generosity of the property owner.

Mack heard of an opening in the maintenance department at General Electric in Peterborough, Ontario and took a trip down to investigate. The company was ramping up production of electrical generators for the construction of the Beauharnois hydroelectric power station along the St. Lawrence Seaway. He got the job, and the family made the journey east.

The position at General Electric was a good one, but as 1939 rolled in, employment prospects at the CPR brightened. Dad was again offered work at the shops. He didn't know it at the time, but his railway job would be without interruption now. This was the beginning of WWII, and the lengthy depression was coming to an end. Munitions and military manufacturing would boom. This would be an expansion that would continue to the end of the war.

There was a good possibility of promotion at GE, so the decision to leave was difficult. It was made easier by the fact that my mother was missing her friends and relatives in Winnipeg. In 1939, they packed their bags, made their way to the rail station in Toronto, and returned to Winnipeg.

The stability of family life returned. Summer life at the cottage in Gimli provided a perfect respite. The steady job and the prospect of continued employment with the railway made for much happiness, but the good fortune changed once again.

Partway into the summer of 1939, my mother became ill. She had a persistent cough and fever. Doctor visits at that time were not covered by a federal health plan, so she postponed seeking medical help. When her health deteriorated further, she had no choice. It was an unwelcome prognosis. She had tuberculosis.

Mom recalled the day she was admitted to the King Edward Hospital in Winnipeg, a forerunner of the current Riverview Health Centre. Her doctor took her package of cigarettes away and told her, "You won't be needing these anymore."

This was a time prior to the invention of penicillin, so rest and sulpha drugs and radical treatments, such as collapsing the lungs, were part of the healing protocol. She took handfuls of sulpha pills. In retrospect, rest was likely the only part of the healing regimen that worked. After over a year in the hospital, she was released with one lung still working. She never regained use of the other lung.

My parents, Madeline and John Mackintosh, with my brother, Ord, in the spring of 1940 in Gimli. Life is looking brighter. Madeline is over her tuberculosis treatment and her dad, John Macdonald, is sailing from Scotland to reside with family in Canada.
Photo from the Mackintosh family collection

Recovering from the disease was the first milestone. Her dad's arrival from Scotland in 1940 was another. Although renting in Winnipeg, they still owned the Gimli cottage—another bit of good fortune. It was indeed a happy time, even though she still had to make monthly visits to the hospital. I assume she was even happier when she discovered her pregnancy in 1941.

The thirties were a decade of troubles for the family. The loss of work for my dad, the loss of the equity in a home for the family and the loss of my mother's health during her crisis with tuberculosis. In retrospect, they were minor concerns.

My brother Duncan died on December 23, 1936.

Retracing Steps

Follow the journey on the map of page iv.

I'm writing a letter to all who remember the good times of Gimli summers.

Dear Friends,

Get a bulldozer!
Let's resurrect the old cabin,
Replant the raspberries,
Construct a cement cooler,
Play ball on the empty lot.
Let the spirit of Spotty live on.

I started at Fifth Avenue today and walked north on Roddy Drive. (Yes, the street that ran by our cottage north from the highway and south to the lake now has a name.) I passed by the Anderson's home on the corner of Sixth. If you remember, that later belonged to the Vann's. Mr. Vann was a talented carpenter. He saved broken hockey sticks and made them into tables. Ours is still around somewhere. Not sure if you know this, but their son, Murray—the black-jacketed Presley look-alike—married the heartthrob of many boys, Bonnie Rudney, Glenn's sister. I recall spending an afternoon assembling her new bicycle. She was even able to ride it afterwards. There was always hope as a fourteen-year-old, especially before Murray made the scene.

The Rudney Store was on the corner of Roddy Drive and the highway. The family lived at the back and operated a grocery store in the front. I assumed that it was the same structure that I knew from our escapades of the fifties, but Glenn reminded me that the building suffered through a fire in the early 1960s and was rebuilt. It's a restaurant now known as MASK.

Glenn and I would be going to the movie theatre and needed first to stock up on snacks. Glenn entered the front door of the store and hollered "Just me." He would pick up a giant pack of sunflower seeds—a necessity—and a pop, perhaps Wynola Cola or Orange Crush, and some bars and candy. All the kids came with sunflower seeds and twenty-five cents to get in. I don't remember anyone buying from the movie confectionary.

The theatre was always packed.

Sometimes you couldn't hear the movie for the cracking and spitting of seeds. Then a guy—never a girl—would roll an empty drink bottle down the aisle—a journey that seemed to take minutes as it clattered and banged down the concrete floor, aided by the odd kick and accompanying chuckles and guffaws. How did anyone ever hear the soundtrack? Sometimes one of the lonely adults in our midst would complain to the owner. The movie would be stopped, and petite and stately Miss Greenberg would appear on the stage. She waited to get the attention of the yahoos and threatened to eject them if they wouldn't comply with the rules. There was reluctant silence. Then, once the reel began to roll, attention to the movie was followed immediately by a resumption of the cracking of seeds. It wasn't long until another bottle rolled down, followed by several more. And then, God Save the Queen which no one observed. People were exiting the side doors as if someone had yelled "Fire." Back on the bikes for the ride home.

Looking back, the film was secondary to the experience. There seemed to be lots of Westerns with continuous action where everything could be solved with guns. Other than *High Noon*, an early 50s film with Gary Cooper, I can't name any others of that genre. *Blackboard Jungle* of 1955 stood out through the din of cracking seeds and rolling bottles. It was maybe the first movie that connected with my personal experience even though the delinquency theme was novel. We too had teachers that had served in WWII but there was generally no nonsense in their classes. Discipline in class was important.

By 1957, Glenn was seldom either around the store or around Gimli. Each day he would travel to Fraserwood—some sixteen kilometres west of Gimli—to be with Gloria, his new girlfriend. It had to be serious. The gravel and rutted hardtop road to Fraserwood wasn't in the best condition, especially for bicycling. But unlike my first summer dating foray, Glenn and Gloria were serious. They were married in 1962 and spent close to fifty-seven years together until Gloria's passing in January 2019.

Johnson Memorial Hospital, Gimli Manitoba as it looked in the fifties.
Photo courtesy of Dilla Narfason

The Johnson Memorial Hospital was on the corner across the street from Rudney's store, replaced now by the Gimli Health Centre: no more cracking of croquet balls, no more shady trees and green grass, no more carriage lights at the entrance, no more circular driveway, and no cackle from the nuns. Life moved on. My sister Marie recalls her early encounter with the hospital and the nuns.

Apparently, my grandmother was a nun, or at least a novitiate at some point, so perhaps this apocryphal story explains my fascination with the nuns I encountered in Gimli. We lived close to the Gimli hospital, but saw them only through the fences as ghostly, gray-swathed figures. They wore long habits and so seemed to float. I could never see their feet and they all seemed in ethereal motion. Where did the nuns live? I thought about that a lot, but never saw them outside of the hospital grounds.

One afternoon, I was trying to infiltrate my brothers' game of baseball in the front yard. My brothers were older and did not let me play, but sometimes I got to be the base or a fan or even the entire fan base for their games. On this particular day, I was somehow an obstruction near the batter. He might deny it, but I think it was Ord who swung the bat; he may or may not have hit the ball, but he smacked me in the arm. I was five, and my wails rivalled the siren at the Gimli Air Force base. I was taken to the hospital. We were met by the mythical nuns, who, up close, were actually motherly and kind. They shepherded me through the X ray process, which in the 1950s was pretty mechanical and scary, but I trusted them implicitly. I thought they were, if not angels, at least close enough to celestial to save me. If they were angels, they were no longer floaty and vague but competent creatures, with faces like my mom's plump friend, or the lady that served ice cream at the Dairy Bar. I was grateful for that, because I needed a loving but human presence. I survived and did not even have a broken arm, although I made the most of my indignity for the folks at home.

Remember the Parrish & Heimbecker grain elevator across the highway from the store? It was demolished maybe twenty years ago—no, probably forty years. I've recalled a structure that was just north of the elevator, a cattle pen. I don't remember it ever being in use, but we would climb it and leap off the roof. Why, you say? Jumping off outhouses and cattle pens was just part of the day.

I turned right at the highway, crossed the ditch, and began walking north along the railway tracks. The old church building, a witness to many marriages of the past, is gone, but there's an attractive new St. Michaels in its place. No bulk oil across the street from the church. No Wye or pond across the tracks.

The Wye was a set of railway tracks in the shape of a Y where the train coming from Winnipeg would back onto one set and take the second set out, ready now to make the journey back to the city. The pond was a deep slough where the water was warm. There was a sturdy log raft on the site. We would come to the pond fully dressed to pole about on the raft, but inevitably end up in the water with the leeches. Rona, the Automatic Car Wash and Sobeys are there now. I wonder who took the raft?

The railway station and water tower are gone now. You're probably wondering where people stand to get on the train? No worries. There are no passenger trains. They ended in the late fifties. The station is gone and so is the water tower.

A little train comes from Winnipeg periodically to pick up whiskey at Diageo. That's where the rail track ends. Yes, there's a distillery north of the town, built by Seagram in 1967.

At the corner of the highway and Centre Street, there's a Co-op Gas station on the site of the former North American Lumber yard. Do you remember when a training aircraft crashed on that site? The NATO pilot had ejected from his smoking plane. Many of the Gimli townsfolk had been watching the saga of the errant craft circling the town. It would have been a lot scarier for folks if they'd known the aircraft was pilotless.

In retrospect, there was a little comedy in putting the fire out after the crash. The RCAF fire fighting crew were on the scene before the Gimli brigade, but the Air Base driver took an alternate route. He decided to cross the field to get close to the fire—a tactic avoided by the local volunteer firefighters, given the boggy nature of the field. The Base fire truck got mired quickly and the fire was out before they were out of the bog—much to the pride of locals and especially Gimli's volunteer firefighting force.

I walked along Centre Street eastward towards the lake to the Canada Post building on the north-east corner of Fifth Avenue. Looking north on Fifth, there's an RCMP depot adjacent to Canada Post. I recall these lots as empty of buildings but edged by enormous spruce trees. There was a clearing in the middle. Occasionally there would be a football scrum. The game would start with two people, but as time passed, others made the scene. There were always enough to have a pick-up game.

Looking east across the lane was Dr. George Johnson's home offset from the corner of Fourth and Centre Street. The yard was always humming with not only birds but also kids and tricycles and the sounds of play. Across the street—looking east on Fourth Avenue—the creek was still running. The Dori Thorkelson family home was set back in the trees along the creek north of Centre Street. Dori had his jeweller's shop on Centre, some 100 metres from his home. The old, renovated shop is now Ship and Plough, a pub and eatery. The creek ran across Centre Street past Slobodian's Second-Hand Store on the south-west corner of Third Avenue and Centre Street. Beverley Einarson knows the history.

Slobodian's Store at Centre and Third Avenue looking south on Third. The store was built to endure the spring floods of the overflowing creek that ran through Gimli.
Photo courtesy of Dilla Narfason

The store at the corner of Third Avenue and Centre Street was built by my grandparents, William Slobodian and Olina Zabinski, in the early thirties. Bill and Olina got started selling second-hand goods, but as time passed, the goods sold were more new than old. To mark the transition, the store was called

"The New and Second-Hand Store." Over time, the "and" of the store name was obliterated from the sign so it read "The New Second-Hand Store." My grandfather ran the store; he sold clothing, dinnerware, materials like thread, blankets, and shoes. People in Gimli always knew when you made a purchase since the goods were wrapped in newspaper and tied with string. Grampa also had a sewing machine and a metal post for shoes, so he was able to fix some of the shoe problems. He also loved fixing clocks. They were all over the store.

After her grandparents died, the responsibilities of the store passed to their daughters. Beverley's mother, Sophie, married to Hannis Kristjanson, and her aunt, Annie, married to Hannis' brother, Ted Kristjanson. Sophie and Annie took turns working the store. That's when I remember my mother and I climbing the steep cement steps—steps that saved the store from the rising creek water of spring.

The creek had its origins in the north-west corner of Gimli, winding its way through the town, beside Thorkelson's Jewelry Shop, then under the wooden pedestrian bridge crossing Centre Street adjacent to Slobodian's Second-Hand Store at Third Avenue and Centre Street (now Flatland Coffee Roasters Café). A culvert facilitated the flow of water under Third Avenue where the creek continued its journey towards Betel Home (close to the present-day New Haven Lodge retirement home at Second Avenue) and out under the breakwater to Lake Winnipeg. Since the inception of the community, spring floods during high water years were a perpetual problem in Gimli. Eventually, in the late 1940s, the town took action and built a ditch from the north-west perimeter of the town to the lake. It's known as the north government ditch. This action reduced the spring flow of the creek and the town flooding during the high spring run-offs of the forties. Then the landfill in the north-west area of Gimli, created by the sewer and water project of 1957, appeared to put the creek permanently underground.

Flooding of the town in the years of high spring-water runoff is no longer an issue, but if you ever have a coffee at Flatland Coffee Roasters, think of the old creek running under your feet.

Remember Central Bakery on the corner of Centre Street and Third Avenue? Who could forget the aroma of fresh bread as we entered the store and the taste of the icing cookies as we left? Dorothy Valgardson provided the details on her dad, Knut, explaining how he arrived in Gimli and subsequently operated the bakery.

This photo, taken in front of Slobodian's Store, looks east on Centre towards the harbour. Central Bakery is the first building on the left, sitting kitty corner to Slobodian's at Third Avenue and Centre Street. The second building looks like Kardy's Hardware. The church building is still on the corner of Second Avenue and Centre Street at the time of this photo.
Photo courtesy of Dilla Narfason

Knut Olsen emigrated from Denmark to Canada in the 1930s to assist his brother, Henry, at Henry's Bakery in St. Vital, a suburb of Winnipeg. He married a Canadian girl, had kids, and in 1940, left the bakery business to join the Royal Canadian Air Force. He served at the Gimli base until the end of the war.

Being a baker, he had his eye on the Dutch Grill, a bakery and café at the corner of Third Avenue and Centre Street. Earlier, it was owned by John Chudd, who had his home and blacksmith shop just down the street. Knut liked living in Gimli, so purchased the business and renamed it Central Bakery in December of 1945. It became a landmark establishment in Gimli, known for its fine bread and Danish pastries.

Dorothy was around ten years of age when she started hanging around the store. Not much later, she was put to work greasing pans and slicing bread. By the age of twelve, Dorothy was serving customers and learning all the intricacies of the retail bakery trade. She still remembers prices from the 1950s.

"Bread unsliced was twelve cents per loaf and thirteen cents sliced. Imperial biscuits sold for forty-five cents, per dozen. There was also a booming business in sweet buns, jam busters, and apple, raisin, and cherry tarts and pies."

One of the greatest innovations of Central Bakery was the early purchase of a rotating oven. This piece of equipment was state of the art and the first such oven sold in Canada. The Beauchemin Brothers, Gimli contractors, installed it. At first, it was a finicky piece, but the brothers kept working on it and eventually had it up to speed. It could bake 360 loaves in one batch and sometimes in the busiest times, there would be three batches a day of brown, rye and Irish bread.

Once the young NATO pilots from Denmark knew that the bakery was run by a Dane, it became their first stop. Knut would bake Danish rye bread and Danish pastries. Better still, it was a chance for the Danes to converse with Knut in their own language.

Dorothy's neighbour, sixteen-year-old Jack Valgardson, was hired to work at the bakery. He soon moved on to other endeavours but stayed close to the Olsen family. Staying close wasn't hard. The year he left the bakery job, Jack married Dorothy.

Sometime in the fifties, a Scottish family, the McSorleys, bought the bakery. They too kept a high standard for their bakery products and maintained the location as the bus depot. Jack Tompkin and I decided it was a great place to stop for a snack and a chat with Miss McSorley—a bonnie lass.

The Noventis Credit Union rests not only on the site of Central Bakery but also on Kardy's Hardware, a business owned by Kardy Gierholm.

Dad would need a metal bracket or odd-sized bolts. If Kardy's didn't have them, there was always Golko's across the street on the south side of Centre. If one store didn't have the product, the other might have. The customer just had to cross the street.

The Golko sign has since been replaced by Lakeview Dental. In a way, this business carried forth the hardware tradition. There are still computers, drills, and sanders, but they are not for sale.

The Lutheran Church used to sit on the corner of Second and Centre. Like the rook of chess, the building moved one lot north towards the movie theatre. The former church building now serves as the Unitarian meeting place and the stage for local summer theatre productions.

On the outside, the old movie theatre building is still intact and looks as it did some sixty-five years ago. There is one change. I planned to pick up a schedule of this month's movies. There weren't any: no postings for the ice box door this year.

As I entered the theatre, I looked over to my left and imagined the past when Bob Thordarson and Carol Eyjolfson would be sitting halfway down that side. They started dating in the early years of junior high. It worked. They are celebrating fifty-nine years of marriage in 2021.

The theatre inside still provides the thrill of cinema, but lacks the chaos of our past. When I took in a movie at the theatre, there wasn't one bottle sent down the aisle during the presentation. No one had to stop the reel and warn the attendees to behave themselves or face the consequences. There was also no anthem at the conclusion of the film. There was one constant from the past. People were making a rapid exit from the side door into the parking lot as the final credits were being shown.

It brought back memories of my first date. I stood at attention that evening for the singing of the anthem so my friends on their bikes would disappear before we exited. We had met at the dock, the lone girl among our school of dolphins. We agreed to meet outside the theatre but when I got there—perhaps I was late—she was inside. I don't think we even had snacks. The time went by too quickly. Maybe the best part was the long walk home, especially with no yahoos on bikes. We had plans to meet again, but that was

55555555

555555555

the summer my dad and I travelled by rail to Vancouver. I was away for three weeks, and on my return, she was gone.

Back on Centre Street, the Gimli Hotel has been painted and has a deck on the east side. No more "Men Only" in the pub, but you can still buy a case of beer at the front door vendor.

I'm here now on the north-west corner of Centre Street and First Avenue, surveying the street and feeling awed at the changes. The HP Tergesen store is still on the corner of First and Centre, looking as it did in the past. I was some ten years of age when my dad took me to the soda fountain for a 7up float. The store has been transformed to become a trendy clothing and gift shop, still a landmark in the commerce of Gimli and a destination for out-of-town shoppers.

Across the street from Tergesen's, there's no chance for a game of pool or the afterwards treat of a toasted pecan bun. Both the pool hall and the Lakeside Café are missing. Gone, too, is the Post Office of old and Olsen's fish store and their menagerie of boats and nets of the fishing trade.

First Avenue, also known as Main Street in earlier times, looking north. The photograph was taken in the late 1940s, perhaps 1948. The Lakeside Trading Company is on the corner, and Sam's Gimli Café is close by. The kids on bikes are heading to the old post office or perhaps the Pier.
Photo courtesy of Mabel Tinguely

The former Lakeside Trading Company stood on the corner lot behind me: an establishment close to my dad's heart. He remembered when it burned to the ground in 1948 or 1949. Dilla Narfason took a job there in the mid-1940s after completing high school and recalls the layout of the store and her responsibilities.

You entered the store from First Avenue. It was referred to as a general merchant establishment divided into two parts. The hardware and building supplies were on one side and the groceries, kerosene, coal oil, embroidery thread, and more was on the other. I got the job as a clerk, serving customers, because I was competent at adding in my head and recording all transactions in the receipt book. But don't ask me to fill kerosene cans. The male clerks could handle that job.

As I walk north on First Avenue, formerly known as Main Street, Sam Toy's Gimli Café was close to the corner. I wish Sam Toy were still around for a chat. I have a lot of questions for him, but isn't life like that? We reach an age where the questions of the past are of interest, but the people who could answer those questions are no longer with us. Fortunately, there are still enough people around who were customers of the restaurant and several who worked for Sam.

It was a dream, owning his own café in Canada, but a lonely one, separated at first from his home and his family and friends, and separated from a different culture and way of life in China.

Finding employees for a restaurant in Gimli was also a challenge. He hired a Chinese cook who lived in Winnipeg. The only problem was his lack of English. It made for some difficulties when conversing with the waitresses. The cook also had to control his temper. His anger leapt out when some of the younger people got under his skin.

Sam was always focused on his customers. He didn't mind the kids hanging around his café. He set up a water fountain so that they could enter at will for a drink. He got to know the youth that hung around outside, realizing that they were both future customers and potential employees. He installed a pinball machine for that purpose. Inevitably, the kids would tilt the machine. He would threaten to ban people from playing if they kept tilting, but I never knew of anyone being banned. The odd purchase of a Coke and chips may have been enough compensation.

The bigger problem was adults, although most customers were decent and respectful. They appreciated a good meal at a good price. They were honest and well-mannered and often told Sam how much they enjoyed the meal. But sometimes there were ignorant people. They entered inebriated, they made too much noise, they were disrespectful to others, and they didn't want to pay.

It must have been a dilemma for Sam. He had to deal with the unruly, but at the same time didn't want to disrupt the enjoyment of others. Sam surely made a contribution to the town by providing reasonably-priced meals and employment for locals, and for supporting others. Evidently, he provided start-up cash for a young tradesman attempting to establish his plumbing business.

Shirley MacFarlane worked as a waitress for Sam in 1950. She recalled his sense of fun and his penchant for sprinkling the green cleaning compound on the floor prior to sweeping.

Mabel Sigurdson Tinguely was only fifteen years of age when she began as a waitress at the Gimli Café in 1948. It was her first job. Mabel recalls the experience.

There were several stools and a counter on one side of the café, and a number of booths on the other. My only concern was with the Chinese cook. He didn't speak any English so to communicate with me he would shout in Chinese. I didn't have a clue what he was saying, but eventually figured it out once I understood the names for the Chinese dishes and worked more shifts. Sam helped me with the translations. The cook was saying,

"This plate of chop suey is ready."

"Take this fried rice now, while it's hot."

"Pick up the bowls of soup."

There was one command that didn't make sense for some time. Then I got it. It didn't relate to the names of the foods.

"Hurry up, people are hungry."

Mabel also observed the difficulties Sam faced with unruly customers. She recalled a time when four young men arrived for supper. They had finished their work for the season and had been celebrating the occasion at the Gimli Hotel. They were highly inebriated when they entered the café. There was a string of racist comments aimed at Sam. They continued to badger Sam, making veiled threats against him. She could tell that Sam was fearful for his safety. He turned pale and shook with anger. He knew he wasn't going to be paid for this meal.

Sam made his way to the cash register and pulled out a thick rubber hose.

I'd never seen Sam so enraged. He returned to the table with his Billy-club weapon at shoulder height and told them to leave immediately.

"Just get out. If not, someone's going to get hurt."

They made a quick exit. The threat of the weapon worked, but Sam was still out of pocket for the four meals.

One day, a guy walked into the café and asked Mabel for a package of Players cigarettes. She stared at him for a minute. She'd never encountered such a good-looking man. The only odd feature was his greying sideburns. Mabel figured he must be too old for her. The young guy kept staring at Mabel, even after she'd brought him the cigarettes. He left the restaurant and Mabel had a sad thought.

"I probably won't see that guy again."

Tip Top Meats, now known as Thai Restaurant and Clothing, was just down the street, north of Sam's Café. I looked in the window past the clothing racks and had a vision of Valdi and Joey, the Arnason boys, who established the business in 1948. There they were behind the counter, meat cleaver at hand, still ready to serve.

And a little further down the street is a low brick building—the past home of the Falcon, the cool-café of First Avenue. There was a diner-style arrangement of stools in the middle, and booths with red leatherette seats along the sides. It was the perfect place to hang out. The Wurlitzer machine was a big attraction. To play a song, you chose the tune and paid for it at your seat. You could keep playing that song all night as long as you continued plugging the machine with nickels. There was seldom silence. If a song was high on the charts, that's all you would hear. The Falcon always hummed, a combination of the music and the sound of the crowd. Every seat was taken. The jukebox wailed; waitresses scrambled; people lined up to get in.

*Shirley MacFarlane, on the left, and her friend, Johanna Renaud Grimolfson,
on the far right, are taking a break from their waitressing jobs at the
Falcon Café. Friends in the middle are unknown.*
Photo courtesy of Shirley MacFarlane

In 1951, after her year with Sam Toy at the Gimli Café, Shirley
MacFarlane took a waitressing job at the Falcon.

*To this day when I hear a Patti Page vocal, I'm back at the
Falcon Café.*

*I also remember when Cecil Luining - a lineman for the Winnipeg
Blue Bombers from 1954 – 1963 - was the delivery person for
Interlake Dairies. After dropping off the order, he would take a seat
and I would make him his favourite milk shake.*

*Lots of us Riverton girls got jobs in Gimli. Fran and Mike Pawlinsky
were the owners of the Falcon at that time. They lived upstairs of the
restaurant. This job was a perfect fit for me. I was enrolled for a business course starting in 1952, and looking for somewhere to stay in
Gimli, so Fran and Mike offered me their extra bedroom.*

*In the evening, the Falcon was a favourite hang-out spot for the
Gimli airmen. There was one group of Scottish pilots that sticks in
my memory. We exchanged names and addresses and would often
receive a card and message from them when they relocated home.*

One of the lads was very quiet. But after graduation from the base and his return to Scotland, he wrote me a letter. He evidently loved his time in Canada and would have gladly returned if the opportunity arose. I sent him a Christmas card that year. Not long afterwards—early 1952 perhaps—I received a letter from his mother. The young pilot had been killed in a night flying accident.

By the way, there's good news for fans of the old Falcon Café. A sign on the building reads "Coming soon, Interlake Brewing."

Brennivins Pizza holds forth half-way down the street. It's just north of the old Town Hall, now the home of Beach Boy Restaurant. Some would remember the site as the centre of local telephone communication. Manitoba Telephone System switchboards hummed.

I stopped for a pizza, their special. I sat by the windows looking out on the east side of First Avenue and tried to imagine what it looked like those many years ago. There was a lone barn-like structure that served as the town bowling alley. Later, it became an ice cream, hamburger, and fries take-out restaurant. Mr. Oakley, the optometrist, had his home and business between the library and the bowling alley. Thanks to Sigurbjorg Stefansson, the quaint library building is still on the corner. An educator and lover of books, Sigurbjorg donated the land that enabled the establishment of a permanent library. Her caveat was that the land could only be used for that purpose. As time passed, her foresight in promoting learning and the joy of reading trumped future commercial developments.

I'm going to head past the corner here where Jacob Greenberg had his store and walk west one block to Second Avenue

Heading north on Second, the limestone building on my left is the former Gimli School. It's now the home of the RM of Gimli, a building no longer connected to a massive fire escape.

Paula Best and her cousin, Valdine, summered with their Amma in a little cottage across the street from the school. They fetched water from the artesian well; they learned to play rummy; they shared stories with each other in the two-holer outhouse and they, too, were big fans of movies at the Gimli Theatre. The school fire escape across from their cottage was their playground. They spent many hours on the arduous climb up and the rapid descent down the winding tube, but not before a call from Valdine's mother.

"Don't rip those jeans—you just got them, you know."

Then, there was another interruption, just when everyone was having the most fun. The custodian would appear to holler at the participants to get off the property. It was always a mystery as to where he was hanging out. Maybe he was cleaning the floors or taking ink marks off desks, keeping busy during the summer months. If the sliders and climbers didn't respond to the order, there was a more urgent command that signalled the end of the fire-escape antics—at least for that day.

I make my way through the playground of the middle school to Fourth Avenue and north through the gates of the Park and Gimli Pavilion.

The Gimli Park and Pavilion in a year prior to cyclonic storms that
often tore through Gimli and the park.
Photo courtesy of Beverley Einarson

It was a busy place on dance nights. Music was wafting through the screened windows, and the dance floor was packed—a mecca of possibilities for young men and women, especially the young women of Gimli, who were interested in the residents of the Air Base. Endless friendships and long-term relationships arose.

Valdine, the former playground climber, and Sigfred, the Norwegian NATO pilot, came dancing here in the early part of their relationship. They had met at a party in Winnipeg. It must have been love at first sight when Valdine said, "I stay at my Amma's in Gimli," and Sigfred said, "I fly T33's in Gimli."

Valdine returned to Gimli, but several weeks passed and no Sigfred. She decided to write him a letter. She addressed the letter to Sigfred Harnes. Unknown to Valdine, his name was pronounced as Harnes but spelled as Hernes. As a result, an unclaimed letter sat pinned for some time on the Base bulletin board. Finally, a pilot colleague said,

"Sigfred, this letter must be for you?"

"You think? But that's not my name."

He opened the letter, and the dancing began.

There were huge groves of mature spruce trees around the Pavilion. They were spaced so that walking through this forest was easy. On moonlit nights, the light would linger in the treetops and illuminate the trails. The shutters around the dance floor were opened, allowing fresh air to flow in and the sounds of music to flow out. Dancers were stamped on the wrist as proof of paying, which led to a continuous flow of people in and out of the dance hall.

There was—and still is—a lip around much of the screened portion of the Pavilion. As a twelve-year-old, I recall driving up to the side, climbing from the seat of my bike onto the lip, and holding the screen to observe the band and the dancers.

Glenn Frain and his Buckaroos often played at the Pavilion. It was a country band. Young Ron Halldorson might be playing steel guitar and Ray St. Germain might be singing. The Men of Note was also a popular attraction in the fifties at the intersection of the fading big band sounds and the advent of rock and roll. Trumpet player Nestor Mudry and saxophonist Glenn Thorsteinson were Winnipeggers who played with the band and were typical of band musicians at that time. They both had day gigs. Playing music was an enjoyable hobby and they were paid for their pleasure. At the height of the band's popularity, they played Wednesday, Friday, and Saturday nights at the Pavilion. If you liked to jive, tango, samba, waltz, and polka all in one night, this was the band for you.

My sister remembers a later era of dancing.

I was a pre-teen when I saw my first movie star in Gimli. He was not actually a movie star, but one of the young European pilots training at the Air Base. He looked like Ed Byrnes "Kookie" from Sunset Strip, and that was enough for me. I knew that if I were ever to meet one of these exotic flyers, I would have to go to a Friday night dance at the Pavilion. On Saturday nights, the Pavilion held dances for the older crowd with bands like Johnny and his Musical Mates. If you were a fan of accordions and fiddles these were your boys. Growing up in a family of accordion playing brothers, it was not my idea of a night out.

By the time I was old enough to go to the Pavilion dances, the air base was closing down and no longer hosted gorgeous young would-be pilots. My dream became simply to dance the night away to the local hot rock band, The Fifth. I knew they were hot because even my city friends had heard of them. We could see the Saints, the Squires, and a Kelvin kid, Neil Young, at the local community centre but the lure of summer nights and the old rustic pavilion trumped the city bands for me.

One summer night, my girlfriend was down from the city, and in a haze of hairspray we began our preparation for the dance. We were finally on our way to the Gimli Pavilion; the place where teenage dreams could come true.

We had danced before, in our rec rooms, our bedrooms and in front of CTV's Dance Party, imitating the moves of those chosen couples. We danced at the high school gym for sock hops and Valentine dances, at the local community centres at the Teen Friday bops; but this was summer and a night of thousand stars. We wore what we thought were amazingly cool jeans and T-shirts with the names of American colleges in graphic design with spotless white sneakers.

Acting as if we had been there many times before, we got the coveted ink stamp on our hands and entered the magic of the Pavilion. The screens were open to the lake-scented night sky, and even if the music boomed through cut-rate speakers, we were transported. The crowd seemed to hold all the beautiful people on the planet. The music was everything we imagined live rock music to be. For us, it was London Palladium or the open-air happenings in Golden Gate Park. Only it was better because we were actually there. We danced with endless partners who pretended to be cool but were as thrilled as we were to be rocking out to the beat that echoed on the wood planked floor. It was both new and eternal.

Walking north past the Pavilion and through the park today is quite a contrast to the past. The thick forest of spruce is gone, thinned by years of heavy cyclonic-type storms—uprooting trees and laying the dance hall bare.

The open field running the length of North Fifth Street is still there. According to signage, this street is called Fifth Avenue North. I've labelled it as a street on my map to avoid confusion with our lots on Fifth Avenue.

I can still feel the jingle of quarters in my jeans after running a race or two at the Icelandic Festival Days. The Ukrainian Orthodox Church is across the street from the park on Fifth Street. I recall being there for Ed Suchy's funeral in 2007.

If I keep walking through Loni Beach, I'm likely to encounter his brother Dave and son Brad tending to lawns. They're still growing a business started when Dave and his brothers, Tony, and Ed, began with a single push mower and a dream of getting paid for their work.

I walk along the sandy shore close to the water's edge. I'm carrying my runners over my shoulder, just for old times' sake. Sometimes I'm on the sand and sometimes in the shallow water. The latent heat from the sand wicks through my feet and body.

The water-smoothed stones caress my soles. The mind, body, and soul merge in renewal as the energy of the earth journeys through my body. The slush of sand dissolves time. Memories flow. I'm back at 132 Fifth, I'm at the pier, I'm on my monster bike, I'm on the pinball machine at Sam's.

Here's where Jack and I observed the drowning. There's a wooden boardwalk now winding from the harbour north. Gimli is still Gimli on the water. Sam's Café is long gone, but Mabel Sigurdson, the waitress at Sam's, now known as Mabel Tinguely, is still here. The guy that walked into Sam's and walked out again came back just over an hour later. He had a beer at the Gimli Hotel pub to find the courage to ask the attractive waitress at Sam's if he could walk her home at the end of her shift. He did just that, and Mabel said "YES."

The young, good-looking guy with the greying sideburns was Roger Tinguely. He was a teletype operator at the Gimli Air Base. They just celebrated their seventieth wedding anniversary.

The dancers, Valdine and Sigfred, were married and returned to Bodø, an Arctic Circle-air base in Norway. After his military career, Sigfred worked as a commercial airline pilot, so the family moved to Copenhagen, Denmark. There's a T33 trainer on a pedestal on First Avenue. Sigfred Hernes visited Gimli some time ago, and sure enough, his logbook confirmed that he had flown that plane.

There are bigger docks and a marina and more pleasure boats. It looks like a famous sea harbour. And, the gas boats are still there, but there's no one playing tag.

Leslie Einarson couldn't recall the exact year of his accident—the fracturing of his arm—but thinks maybe 1951–52. He was on the breakwater, the same rock structure that we traversed as a family to reach our swimming spot on the beach. It was a great place to play. Several trees were overhanging the shore, and the boys were climbing. Les came out of the trees and started wrestling with a friend. He lost his balance and tumbled onto the rocks. He heard his arm crack. It was a nasty fall. He was taken to the Gimli

Hospital and X rays confirmed the breaks—the wrist, elbow, and further up. The doctor put on a cast. Then there was pain; the cast felt too tight. He was back to the doctor. It didn't look good, so Les was driven to the Children's Hospital and admitted. His roommate was from Riverton. The lad had been kicked by a horse and was unconscious. To Les, the boy appeared to have a much more serious injury. But the prognosis for Les was not good. Gangrene had set in, so surgery was required. Les lost his arm at the shoulder.

Back in Gimli, Les remembered the kindness of his former teacher, Mrs. Thorsteinson. She visited regularly, kept him up to speed with schoolwork and encouraged him in his convalescence. By the next summer, he was riding his bicycle and swimming at the pier and saving those over their heads at risk of drowning—all with one arm.

I wasn't around for my family's turmoil of the thirties and the tragedy of my brother Duncan's death. In retrospect there was a lot of the "bitter" and not much of the "better." Ord was only two and a half when our brother disappeared from his life. You don't remember much at that age, but Ord does recall Duncan's laugh and his love of roughhousing. They were undoubtedly close play-mates. It was well into the late fifties before I heard the snippets of conversation about my brother's short life. I had no idea of the cause of his death.

I was also unaware of our family's story of the thirties: the lack of work, the moves, the sickness, and the sacrifices inherent in holding on to the Gimli cottage. I took our summers in Gimli for granted. The place was always there. We came every summer. It was part of our being. I was one lucky guy. It's a good part of the reason for telling this story, putting the happy memories to word, and remembering a brother I'd never met. I knew that Duncan had died prior to my birth, but my mother never explained the causes of his death or her personal suffering. She buried the details deep in her being.

I was nineteen years of age, on a trip with my brother, Ord, to the Seattle World Fair in 1961. We stopped in Vancouver to visit the Reays who had lived next door to my parents on Garfield Street when Duncan died on December 23, 1936. They spoke of the anguish and heartbreak of the occasion, the distraught state of my mother and their memories of wee Ord staying with them over these times.

In the first two years of Duncan's life, everything appeared normal. He was learning to walk like any other child. There were no worries. And then in the third, he developed a gait, a swinging out of his legs to get his balance; sometimes stumbling as his legs gave way. But he was still full of life; holding a hammer to help his mother build the little bridge over the ditch on Fifth Avenue and rolling on the floor with Spotty, the fox terrier pup.

In 2006, I retrieved Duncan's death certificate. The immediate cause of death was broncho pneumonia, but the other morbid condition contributing to the death was pseudo hypertrophic muscular paralysis, the medical name as of 1936 for this scourge. The condition is now known as Duchene's muscular dystrophy. Duncan's muscles were not developing in a normal manner. His body was missing a key ingredient—the protein dystrophin— and there was no way to supplement that ingredient. The lack of muscle formation in his chest meant that he couldn't cough up the phlegm from the pneumonia. The lack of muscle formation in his legs meant that eventually, he couldn't walk.

Muscular dystrophy is a genetic disorder. Females carry the mis-formed gene, but are not subject to the disease. Males get the disease at birth when the faulty gene makes its way into the DNA. It's a lottery. My brother and I won that lottery. We received two healthy dystrophin-producing genes and didn't contract muscular dystrophy.

Lake Winnipeg—Manitoba's North Sea—some 482 kilometres long and 161 kilometres across at its widest, is more like an ocean, not only in how it looks but also in how it acts. There's no guarantee of seeing across to the other side some twenty (thirty-two km) miles east of Gimli. The lake is often tranquil—placid even—and inviting, coaxing you in for cooling on a hot day. But there's another side, a side with a temper. Because of the shallow depth of the water, the waves of this lake are ferocious when the water is roiled and upset by nasty weather. The gale force winds, the rain, the dark clouds, the lightning flashes, and the cannons of thunder force a move to shelter. Such a frenzy can send the best sailors ashore.

The Icelandic sagas have lingered, floating in from the harbour and hanging over the village, persevering, like the early settlers, determined to survive from fishing the lake with their skiffs of summer and their ice-augers of winter. And farther west from the lake, a different settler and his family laboured to work the land, scrabbling to grow a crop from stony, infertile, and uncooperative soil. They were Eastern Europeans, many Ukrainians and Poles who faced harsh winters and difficult conditions.

Their spirits, too, live on in this town, hiding in the whistling poplars and traversing the forests—spirits transported by the rich flocks of songbirds and the trickster blue jays.

It doesn't take much wondering to understand why people have stayed in Gimli or why they moved back in their retirement. It's the same reason that took people to Gimli in the first place. It's Lake Winnipeg, that enormous body of water with its own realm of power. The lake compels us to absorb the vast sweep of the horizon; it tempts us to dip in toes and to feel the grip of most recent ice; it nourishes us with lungs full of fresh air; it restores the child in us.

In 1957, the town of Gimli passed a motion to begin the process of installing sewer and water. My mother was keen on the idea, but my dad, not so much. The cottage was old and small. Construction of an addition to support sewer and water facilities would need to happen at a cost that would exceed the value of the present cottage. In 1957, property was purchased on Lake Winnipeg some four kilometres north of the town. Construction of a new cottage began, and we moved north in 1958. The two barrels, Hot and Cold, were reinstalled to capture rainwater and to perpetuate a notion of comfort.

In 1997, the Macdonald side of the family had their first reunion in Gimli. My cousin, Ken, and his wife, Marion, were there. Here's a photo of the family at that event. My mother, Madeline, was ninety years of age that year. After those turbulent early years, she died in 2009 in her 103rd year of life. My dad passed on in 1973.

Joe Mackintosh

From the left,
Back Row: Jody Gordon; Ord Mackintosh; our son, John Mackintosh;
Gerry Gordon
Middle Row: Rod Gordon; Madeline Mackintosh; Marion Macdonald;
my sister, Marie Gordon; my wife, Carole Mackintosh
Front Row: Ken Macdonald; our daughter, Karen Mackintosh; Caitlin Gordon;
our daughter, Heather Mackintosh; Joe Mackintosh
Photo from the Mackintosh family collection

Bibliography

Author's journal

Gimli Saga, 1975. Published by the Gimli Women's Institute

Gimli Memories, 1982, a compilation of significant Gimli milestones by Dilla Narfason and Mary Shebeski

Those Were the Days, 2014, a pictorial history of Winnipeg Beach by Wally Johannson

Baldur's Song, a novel by David Arnason, 2010, published by Turnstone Press

Acknowledgments

Many thanks to those who helped get this book to publication.

After an early draft of writing, Jordan Wheeler, the 2018–19 Writer in Residence at the Winnipeg Public Library, provided helpful advice.

To supplement the accuracy of my memory, I used information as direct quotes from the following long-time Gimli residents: Beverley Einarson, Dorothy Valgardson, Leslie and Elaine Einarson, Dilla Narfason, Shirley MacFarlane, and Mabel Tinguely. My sister, Marie, provided her memories of visiting the old Gimli Hospital and dancing at the pavilion. I knew her superb writing skills would enhance any book.

Others: Jack Tompkin, Donna Goodman, Glenn Rudney, Bob Thordarson, Dave Suchy, Paula Best, Valdine Hernes, Solange Liang, Cheryl and Ross Bailey, David Arnason and Lorna Tergesen provided additional stories and often confirmation of my recollections, saving me from the "You're making it up" accusation.

My son-in-law, Anthony Woodward, a talented graphic artist, took my rough drawing of the town of Gimli in the fifties and created the map of Gimli.

My brother, Ord, contributed his memories and a trove of photographs of our family at Gimli. Dilla Narfason, Beverley Einarson, Mabel Tinguely and Shirley MacFarlane shared their photos of what Gimli looked like in earlier years. Professional photographer, Jana Wenzel, worked on a number of the black and white images, improving the quality in the process.

As usual, Karen and Josh, Heather and Anthony, and John and Erin provided encouragement and critiques of the manuscript, especially in the early stages. Given her expertise in both writing and editing, Karen was an invaluable source of help.

Helen Norrie read an early version of the story. Her comments shaped the final product. She also provided guidance with suggestions for improving and correcting my punctuation. I should have paid more attention in my ninth-grade grammar classes.

Thanks to Carole, who has provided unwavering support for all my writing adventures.

Printed in Canada